D1564268

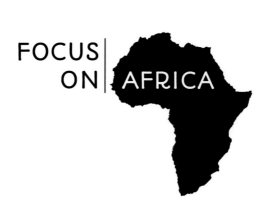

FOCUS ON AFRICA

Health in Contemporary Africa

Derek L. Miller

Cavendish Square

New York

Published in 2017 by Cavendish Square Publishing, LLC
243 5th Avenue, Suite 136, New York, NY 10016

Website: cavendishsq.com

This publication represents the opinions and views of the author based on his or her personal experience, knowledge, and research. The information in this book serves as a general guide only. The author and publisher have used their best efforts in preparing this book and disclaim liability rising directly or indirectly from the use and application of this book.

CPSIA Compliance Information: Batch #CW17CSQ

All websites were available and accurate when this book was sent to press.

Library of Congress Cataloging-in-Publication Data

Names: Miller, Derek L.
Title: Health in contemporary Africa / Derek L. Miller.
Description: New York : Cavendish Square Publishing, 2017. | Series: Focus on Africa | Includes index.
Identifiers: ISBN 9781502623775 (library bound) | ISBN 9781502623782 (ebook)
Subjects: LCSH: Public health--Africa. | Health planning--Africa. | Health status indicators--Africa.
Classification: LCC RA545.M55 2017 | DDC 362.1096--dc23

Editorial Director: David McNamara
Editor: Caitlyn Miller
Copy Editor: Michele Suchomel-Casey
Associate Art Director: Amy Greenan
Designer: Amy Greenan
Production Assistant: Karol Szymczuk
Photo Research: J8 Media

Printed in the United States of America

Contents

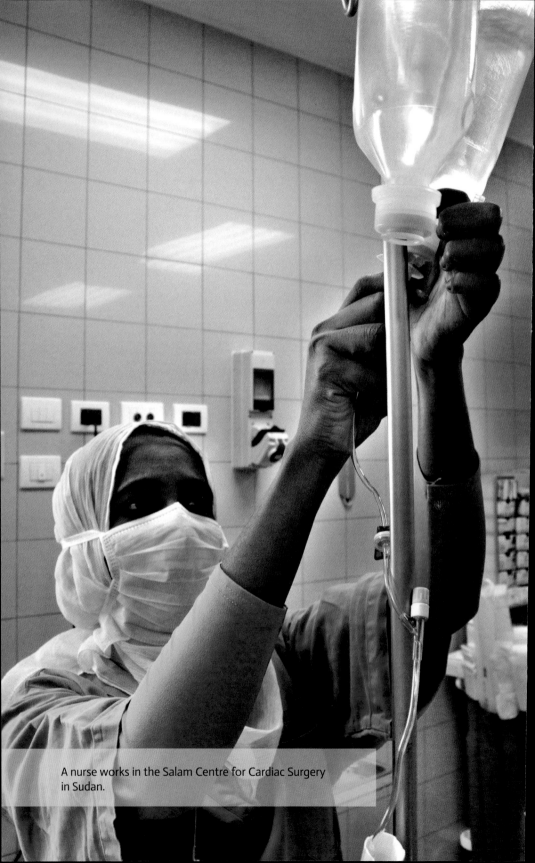

A nurse works in the Salam Centre for Cardiac Surgery in Sudan.

Progressing Toward Health

When people think about health in Africa, many things come to mind: the HIV/AIDS epidemic, the recent Ebola outbreak, malaria, hunger, and poverty. But the reality is that health care in Africa is expanding. People are living longer, more productive lives. Many diseases are being combated effectively. Other diseases have even been eradicated in recent years.

Since 1990, great strides have been made across the continent. The infant **mortality rate** fell by 40 percent between 1990 and 2014, and the maternal mortality rate fell by more than 40 percent as well. While these might sound like abstract numbers, this means millions of children and mothers are alive today who would have died in the past from inadequate health care. There have also been advances in the fight against the diseases and epidemics that plague the region: HIV/AIDS, malaria, and **tuberculosis**. These diseases are still responsible for many deaths across the continent, but they are not spreading as quickly as they have in the past. In particular, the transmission of HIV from mother to child has dropped dramatically due to more effective treatments and outreach to vulnerable populations.

Despite these gains in recent years, much progress remains to be made on the continent. Compared to the rest of the world, child and maternal mortality rates remain high. Access to safe drinking water and food are perennial areas of concern, even though these too have improved in recent years. Unsafe drinking water and malnutrition still kill millions of Africans every year. Health care services are often limited, and many countries suffer from a shortage of qualified health care workers. Even when health care is available, it is sometimes out of reach for those living in poverty. There are more than a million **displaced people** (or refugees) in Africa—people who have been forced to flee their home because of violence. Refugees living in camps are especially vulnerable to many diseases because of cramped conditions and inadequate sanitation—both increase the transmission of diseases.

Africa is an extremely diverse continent. Made up of fifty-four countries, it is home to more than a billion people who speak more than a thousand different languages. Some of the most populous cities in the world, such as Lagos, Nigeria, are in Africa, but a huge number of people still live in rural areas with limited access to modern health care. Various diseases are **endemic** to different regions, and the governments of the African countries vary widely in their handling of the issue of health care. Some governments prioritize stopping the spread of diseases, while others spend very little money on the issue.

The **African Union (AU)**, an international organization of every country in Africa (except Morocco), divides the continent into five regions: northern, western, central, eastern, and southern Africa. Each region is home to a number of countries. In this book, we will examine each region in turn and look at the state of health care in various countries. In each chapter, we will take an in-depth look at one major disease on the continent, one **neglected tropical disease**, and one topic relating to conflict and health. In the last chapter of the book, we will look to the future of the continent. There are many reasons to be hopeful, especially with the rise of technology. It is likely that people in rural communities will be able to access health care in ways we have never seen before. Advances like drones and video conferencing are poised to change the face of health care in Africa—and internationally. But there will also be challenges in the future. Global warming may cause the spread of some diseases and also lead to greater food insecurity and more frequent water shortages. One thing is for sure: health in Africa is changing at a rapid pace, and these changes affect us all.

The Great Pyramids lie just outside the bustling city of Cairo.

Northern Africa

1

Northern Africa is made up of six countries: Algeria, Egypt, Libya, Mauritania, Morocco, and Tunisia (as well as one disputed country, the Sahrawi Republic). It is bordered by the Mediterranean Sea to the north, which lies between Europe and Africa. The Sahara Desert covers much of the southern portion of the region, but most people live north of the desert in a thin band of land near the Mediterranean Sea, where the climate is much less extreme.

Northern Africa is somewhat of an outlier on the continent. It has close ties to the Middle East, linguistically and culturally, and many differences from the rest of Africa. In fact, when academics talk about Africa, they often refer to sub-Saharan Africa (every region excluding northern Africa) while northern Africa is grouped with the Middle East, forming the MENA region (Middle East and North Africa). It makes good sense to talk about the MENA region in certain contexts. For example, the **Arab Spring**—the wave of protests and uprisings that began in 2010—swept across northern Africa *and* the Middle East. Therefore, many scholars discuss the Middle East and northern Africa together when they talk about this topic.

Bacteria Versus Viruses

Bacteria and viruses can both make us sick, but they are very different things. Bacteria are single-celled organisms. Most bacteria exist outside of a living host, but some cause diseases when they live inside of a person or animal. On the

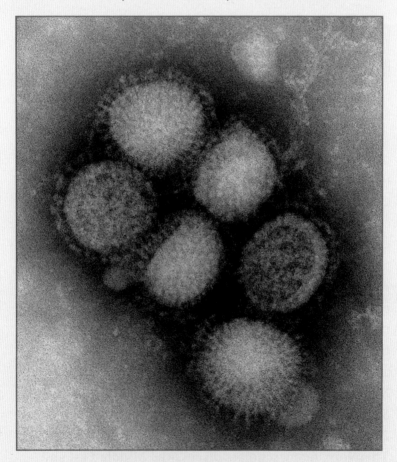

Viruses, like this H1N1 influenza virus, need a living host.

other hand, viruses are smaller than a single cell. For their continued existence, therefore, they require a living cell from a host to replicate in. Or something similar. In fact, this means that viruses are not even considered living organisms because they cannot reproduce on their own.

Some diseases, like tuberculosis and strep, are caused only by bacteria. Others, like AIDS and the flu, are caused only by viruses. Still, other diseases, like pneumonia, may result from viruses or bacteria. The fact that viruses and bacteria are different is critical to their treatment. Bacterial infections are treated with antibiotics, and viral infections are treated with antiviral drugs.

Historically, there was sometimes confusion over whether a disease was caused by a bacteria or a virus. One such case is yellow fever, a disease that still exists in Africa and once plagued North and South America as well. Scientists at the beginning of the twentieth century debated whether the disease was caused by a bacteria or a virus for decades. Finally, Max Theiler, a South African researcher, proved that a virus caused the disease. He later developed a **vaccine** for yellow fever and became the first African to win a Nobel Prize for this breakthrough.

Health in Northern Africa

Northern Africa leads the continent in many ways when it comes to health care. It has the highest average life expectancy of any region in Africa. Maternal, infant, and child mortality rates are relatively low in the region. Access to health care and clean drinking water is widespread, and malnutrition is uncommon. The region has so far avoided the HIV/AIDS and malaria epidemics that confront the rest of the continent to varying degrees. But the picture is not entirely bright. In Tunisia, the health care system is facing a number of challenges related to funding and equal access to care. Other pressing problems also face the region. The Arab Spring ignited conflicts that continue to rage, especially in Libya, which is in the midst of a civil war. The Libyan health care system, once a leader on the continent, is now in shambles.

Average Life Expectancy

The average life expectancy in northern Africa is quite high compared to other regions of Africa. This is partially due to the rarity of HIV/AIDS and malaria, as well as better access to health care. In northern Africa, average life expectancy is just over seventy years; by comparison, it is seventy-eight years in the United States. While that may seem like a large difference, average life expectancy throughout much of Africa is far lower than seventy years. For example, in the region of southern Africa, average life expectancy is just fifty-one years (according to the African Development Bank). Relatively low rates of maternal and infant mortality are another reason for the high average life expectancy of northern Africa.

Maternal Mortality

According to the **World Health Organization (WHO)**, "Complications during pregnancy and childbirth are a leading cause of death and disability among women of reproductive age in **developing countries**" (another term for low-income countries). This is because pregnancy and childbirth present a number of risks to the health of the mother, including **postpartum** (meaning after birth) bleeding, postpartum infection, and obstructed labor (when the baby cannot pass through the pelvis and be born during labor). Though these risks are serious and can lead to death, they are relatively easy for skilled medical practitioners to treat. This is why maternal death is common in developing countries but uncommon in **developed countries** (or high-income countries). Women in developed countries generally have greater access to medical care than those in developing countries.

The maternal mortality rate in northern Africa is very low for the continent (and the world), with the exception of Mauritania. Relatively widespread access to health care means mothers are likely to receive medical treatment if there are complications during pregnancy or childbirth. In fact, the maternal mortality rate is lower in Libya than in the United States. In the rest of the countries of the region, the rate is higher than the United States but significantly lower than that of sub-Saharan Africa.

Child Mortality

Like maternal mortality rates, infant and child mortality rates in northern Africa are significantly lower than in the rest of the continent. In sub-Saharan Africa, one in ten children die before seeing their fifth birthday. But throughout most of northern Africa, fewer than one in fifty children below the age of five die. Northern Africa's success in battling child mortality is due to a number of factors. The widespread use of vaccines combats many infectious diseases that kill children. The absence of malaria (the second most common reason for deaths of children under five around the world) is also a contributing factor. Lastly, relatively low rates of malnutrition in northern Africa result in a lower risk of death. According to the WHO, malnutrition is a contributing cause of death in nearly half of under-five deaths. Survivable diseases can often become fatal in people suffering from malnutrition.

Noncommunicable Diseases

Cause of death can be due to one of three things: communicable diseases (such as bacteria and viruses), **noncommunicable diseases** (like cancer and heart disease), and injury (such as murder, suicide, and accidents). In developed countries like the United States, the vast majority of deaths are due to noncommunicable disease. This is because most communicable diseases can be treated or prevented with access to high-quality medical care. As a result, most people live until a noncommunicable disease eventually takes their life. In contrast, communicable diseases are responsible for the majority of deaths throughout sub-Saharan Africa and other developing regions. Even though these deaths are preventable, there is insufficient medical infrastructure to do so in these regions. Noncommunicable diseases are responsible for relatively few deaths in sub-Saharan Africa because most people do not live long enough for diseases like heart disease to become a fatal.

However, in northern Africa, noncommunicable diseases are a serious public health problem. This is because of the higher average life expectancy of the region compared to the rest of the continent. Heart disease is a leading cause of death in the region (as it is in the United States, but unlike the rest of the African continent). In this way, the region has more in common with developed nations than with the rest of the African continent, where communicable diseases are the primary concern.

Infectious Disease

When you think of infectious diseases you might think of the diseases that dominate the headlines: the Ebola virus (which killed fewer than fifteen thousand people) or avian flu (with a death toll of fewer than one thousand). While these diseases do present a risk if they spread, they are responsible for relatively few deaths historically. The real killers of mankind are not the ones that grab headlines. They are the ones that we rarely hear about: tuberculosis, diarrheal diseases, malaria, pneumonia, and AIDS (once a popular headline but now rarely talked about). All of these kill hundreds of thousands (or millions) of people each year. While it may be hard for us to imagine dying from a disease that can now be prevented with a vaccine, like tuberculosis, or something that is not fatal with even the most basic medical care, like diarrhea, these diseases affect billions of people in developing countries—killing millions every year. Africa is one of the most seriously affected continents by all of these diseases.

Malaria and HIV/AIDS

As we have seen, northern Africa has important geographic and cultural differences from sub-Saharan Africa. Because of its relative geographic isolation, separated from the rest of the continent by the Sahara Desert, it is also an anomaly when it comes to the infectious diseases that affect the region. Malaria and HIV/AIDS—two of the most common causes of death in Africa—are rare in northern Africa. HIV/AIDS is more common at the southern extreme of the continent, and rates generally decline the farther north one looks. In fact, most countries in northern Africa have a lower prevalence of HIV than the United States. For instance, the prevalence of HIV in Algeria is only 0.1 percent of the population, while it is over 0.3 percent in the United States. Compare this to South Africa, where the HIV rate is over 18 percent of the population. From these figures, we can see that HIV/AIDS—the leading cause of death in Africa—is uncommon in northern Africa. Additionally, malaria—the fourth leading cause of death on the continent—is not a problem for most of northern Africa due to the climate and eradication campaigns in the past that proved successful. Thus, two of the most deadly diseases in Africa are largely absent from northern Africa.

Tuberculosis

Tuberculosis (TB), AIDS/HIV, and malaria are often considered the three major infectious diseases of the African continent. Unlike AIDS/HIV and malaria, TB is prevalent throughout northern Africa. It is a major public health concern, and it afflicts the region to a much greater degree than it does highly developed nations like the United States or Canada. After HIV/AIDS, TB is the infectious disease that kills the most people around the world: approximately 1.5 million people each year die from it.

TB is a bacterial infectious disease. Caused by the bacterium *Mycobacterium tuberculosis*, it most often affects the lungs. In an otherwise healthy person who is infected with

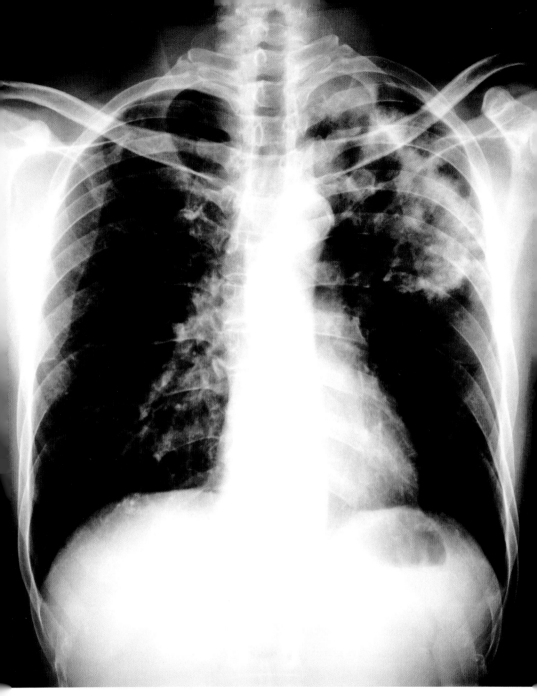

X-rays are used to diagnose cases of tuberculosis.

TB, there are commonly no symptoms because the immune system isolates the disease in the body. Such a person is not contagious and is said to have latent TB. According to the WHO, one-third of the world's population has latent TB. While these people are asymptomatic and cannot transmit the disease, they are at risk for developing active TB in the future.

Approximately 10 percent of people with latent TB will developed active TB during their lifetimes. The most common form of active TB is pulmonary TB (or TB affecting the lungs). But extrapulmonary TB (TB outside the lungs) is also possible if the bacteria travel to other areas of the body. The symptoms of all forms of active TB can include fatigue, fever, weight loss, weakness, and night sweats. Symptoms of pulmonary TB include a severe cough, coughing up blood, and chest pain. The symptoms of extrapulmonary TB depend on where the bacteria is located: common places are bones and lymph nodes. When the bacteria is present in lymph nodes, swelling is the most common symptom. When it is present in bones, it usually causes pain and sometimes makes the bones brittle and more prone to breaking. TB is spread through the air when a person with active TB coughs, sneezes, speaks, or does any other activity that expels tiny droplets that carry the bacteria. It is not easily transmitted, and most infections result from prolonged, close contact with an infected person. Almost half of people with active TB will die from the disease if it is not treated. Death becomes almost certain in conjunction with AIDS.

Despite the fact that tuberculosis kills a million and a half people a year, it is curable. Since it is a bacterial disease, antibiotics are an effective treatment. But it is necessary to take antibiotics for six to nine months to cure TB, much longer than is typical for other infections. Because symptoms of TB disappear relatively quickly, some patients stop taking their medication before they are supposed to. This can cause the TB to reoccur in the patient and be resistant to treatment. The occurrence of multidrug-resistant TB is a serious global health threat. As strains of bacteria gain resistance to common antibiotics, they become harder to cure. While there are fears this may result in a drug-resistant TB epidemic in the future, most strains of multidrug-resistant TB are found in Asia and Russia, not Africa.

In addition to being curable, there is also a vaccine for TB: the Bacille Calmette-Guérin (BCG) vaccine. While it is the most frequently administered vaccine in medical history, it does not provide complete protection from the disease. In fact, the WHO states "there is no substantial evidence that BCG reduces the risk of becoming infected with [TB]." What the vaccine does do is prevent severe cases of the disease in children and infants. But even this protection fades with age. While the BCG vaccine is widely used today, there is a concerted effort to develop a more effective vaccine that could protect adults or completely prevent transmission of the disease.

Neglected Tropical Diseases and Trachoma

The WHO defines neglected tropical diseases (NTDs) as "a diverse group of communicable diseases that prevail in tropical and subtropical conditions in 149 countries and affect more than one billion people, costing developing economies billions of dollars every year. They mainly affect populations living in poverty, without adequate sanitation and in close contact with infectious **vectors** [commonly insects] and domestic animals and livestock." Thus, NTDs are vector-borne diseases: they are spread by a living organism (or vector) that transmits the disease to humans. Common vectors include insects, such as mosquitoes, flies, or ticks, as well as livestock. These diseases are neglected because they primarily affect people living in poverty in low-income countries, a population that is often not prioritized by governments or international organizations.

Some of these diseases can be fatal, but many cause disability and suffering rather than death. One such disease is trachoma. It, unlike most NTDs, is present in northern Africa (which does not have a tropical climate). Trachoma is an infectious disease caused by a bacterium that afflicts the eyes. It leads to scarring on the inside of the eyelids, and left untreated this can result in blindness as the rough scars rub against the surface of the eye. An estimated half a million people around the world are irreversibly blind from the disease, and almost two million are less seriously affected but still visually impaired. In fact, the disease is so prevalent the WHO states that 1.4 percent of all human blindness around the world is due to trachoma.

The disease is easily treatable with antibiotics in its early stages and then surgery when the damage is still reversible. But the communities that suffer from trachoma often do not have access to medical care. As a result, these communities, often some of the poorest in the world, also lose an estimated $8 billion a year in productivity due to visual impairment.

Conflict and Health: Violence

When we think of the danger that war poses, we often think of weapons of mass destruction: nuclear bombs, chemical weapons, and biological agents. But these weapons have rarely been used in the last seventy years since World War II ended. In reality, the greatest killer in modern warfare is small arms: handguns, rifles, machine guns, land mines, and grenades. These weapons can be used to devastating effect

Assault rifles and rocket-propelled grenades like those pictured above have killed many more people than weapons of mass destruction.

by untrained soldiers (including the hundreds of thousands of child soldiers fighting in the world today). In the WHO report *Small Arms and Global Health*, Suzanne Bickerstaffe, a registered nurse, describes the violence that gunshots inflict on the human body:

> Regardless of what happens to our heroes on TV, gunshots are rarely neat, clean, predictable and restricted to "flesh wounds." When a bullet enters the body, it's a spinning missile. The amount of damage and relative size of the entrance and exit wounds depends on many factors: the calibre of the bullet, the distance from the victim when fired, and the organs, bone, blood vessels and other structures hit.

Striking bones causes the bullet to become misshapen, flattening out. The bone shatters, creating splinters that themselves can become lethal weapons, and altering the path of the bullet in an unpredictable manner. Sometimes the final resting place of the bullet in the body or the place where it exits is very unexpected. As a general rule, exit wounds are larger than entrance wounds—sometimes inches larger, if the bullet's shape has become distorted by the structures hit.

An estimated three hundred thousand people around the world die each year due to small arms. Nearly a third of these deaths are during armed conflicts (the remainder are murders or suicides). Armed conflicts are currently taking place in a number of African countries, including Nigeria, Somalia, Sudan, South Sudan, and Libya. In northern Africa, the civil war in Libya is the largest armed conflict—violence has claimed tens of thousands of lives in Libya since 2011, when longtime dictator Muammar Ghaddafi sparked a civil war by violently putting down protests that were part of the Arab Spring. The conflict still rages there, and there is no end in sight.

Death by violence is the most obvious effect that conflict has on human health. But conflict also affects people in indirect ways. It forces people from their homes, often depriving them of clean water and health care. It leaves a legacy of violence in the minds of those who live through conflict, on the bodies of people who are crippled by injury, and in the very earth where the conflict occurred as concealed land mines kill and maim civilians for generations to come. We will examine these further consequences of conflict in the coming chapters.

Tunisia: A Model for the Continent

The Universal Declaration of Human Rights, a document adopted by the United Nations, states that "Everyone has the right to a standard of living adequate for the health and well-being of himself and of his family, including food, clothing, housing and medical care and necessary social services." This notion that health is a human right—something that all humans should be guaranteed no

In recent years, Tunisia has been known for its citizens' protests, including the Arab Spring.

matter their circumstances in life—is all too often ignored by governments around the world. Sometimes, medical care is too expensive for people to afford. Other times, people simply have no access to medical care because the nearest clinic is too far from their home.

But Tunisia takes the human right to health care seriously. It is enshrined in its constitution, which was adopted in 2014, after the Arab Spring swept the previous government out of power. The constitution states, "Health is a right for every human being. The state shall guarantee preventative health care and treatment for every citizen and

The Eradication of Malaria

Today, people often think of malaria as a tropical disease—common in rain forests and other hot, wet climates. But malaria used to be endemic to much of the world, including the United States and Europe. In the past, we know that is was quite common in Europe: Shakespeare refers to it repeatedly in his plays (by the name "ague"), and it was only in 1951 that malaria was eradicated in the United States. At the present time, malaria is indigenous to parts of Africa, South and Central America, Asia, and Oceania, but this containment is a relatively recent occurrence.

As European powers colonized Africa, they began to combat malaria in the African colonies. Malaria is spread by certain species of mosquitoes, so efforts to eradicate malaria revolved around controlling the population of these mosquitoes. In order to do this, a number of measures were used: standing water (the breeding ground for mosquitoes) was minimized, DDT (a powerful insecticide) was sprayed on water and in homes, and drugs that prevent transmission (such as quinine) were distributed. In some regions, these efforts were unsuccessful, but in northern Africa a great deal of progress was made: the climate in the region is unfavorable for malaria, and the Sahara Desert forms a natural barrier to mosquitoes. Although malaria was still present in northern Africa as the countries of the region gained their independence from the European powers, the disease was soon eradicated. Tunisia was declared malaria-free in 1979, and over the next decades Egypt, Libya, Algeria, and Morocco were as well. (It is still endemic to Mauritania—the southernmost of the countries in northern Africa.)

provide the means necessary to ensure the safety and quality of health services." Health care is almost universally accessible to everyone. The Tunisian government offers free or nearly free health care to low-income families—nearly a third of the country's population

Currently, Tunisia is a leader on the continent with regard to health care. The average life expectancy of a person in Tunisia is seventy-five years. This is the highest average life expectancy on the continent of Africa, and it is more than twenty years higher than some countries on the continent. The long life of Tunisians is due to the priority that the government has placed on health care throughout the nation's history. A series of vaccination campaigns and improvements in sanitation and access to clean water cut down on the spread of infectious diseases throughout the country. Across many countries, health care is still hard to come by in rural, low-income areas. But beginning in the 1980s in Tunisia, the government prioritized bringing health care to remote areas, and average life expectancy rose as a result. While inequalities still exist (the average life expectancy is higher in large cities), the government is committed to addressing them and health care across the country—even in rural and low-income areas—is accessible and high-quality.

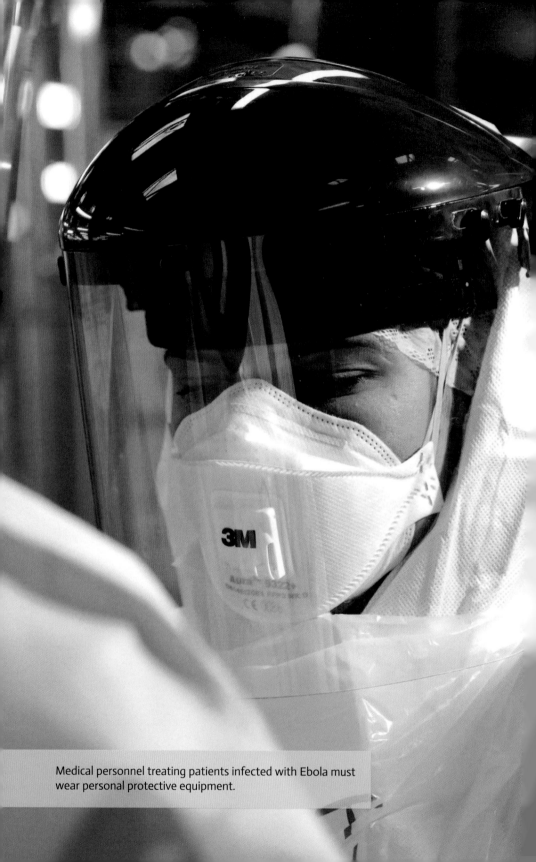

Medical personnel treating patients infected with Ebola must wear personal protective equipment.

2 | Western Africa

The diversity of western Africa is astonishing. It is home to fifteen countries and more than five hundred different languages. Unlike northern Africa—where the governments of the region primarily use the Arabic language—the governments of western Africa use French or English, depending on which country was formerly the colonial power. Even the geography of the region spans a huge range, from the Sahara Desert in the north to dense rain forests in the south.

The people of the region are also quite diverse. In addition to speaking hundreds of different languages, they have very different customs and traditions. There are many Muslims and Christians as well as followers of traditional African religions. The wealth of the region also varies. **Per capita gross domestic product (GDP)** is a measure of the total wealth a country creates in a year divided by the number of people who live there. The result is the average income of a person in the country (if that wealth were divided equally). In the small western African island nation of Cabo Verde, the per capita GDP was $3,131 in 2015, while in Niger it was only $359. Such a large disparity in wealth has consequences on the health care systems of different countries.

Colonization

The colonization of the Americas and Africa by European countries has played an enormous role in human history and continues to affect the world we live in. It was responsible for the fall of great civilizations, like the Aztecs and Incas, and the founding of today's superpower: the United States. It is why English—the language of a small European island—is used to communicate around the world in places as distant as Canada, Australia, and South Africa. It is also why many indigenous people around the world no longer exist because they were killed by disease and European conquerors. Their languages and cultures are forever lost.

The Door of No Return on Gorée Island—the last sight of Africa for many slaves who were forced to leave their homeland

Colonization also had monumental effects on health around the world. Diseases that were once isolated in small areas spread around the globe. Carried by European colonists and African slaves, these diseases killed hundreds of millions of people, and they still exist today in locations where they were not endemic in the past. Some diseases from Africa and Europe spread to the Americas, while other diseases spread from the Americas to Africa and Europe. The European colonization of Africa ended during the second half of the twentieth century, but the effects are still seen today. Many African countries use European languages for governance, and the political instability of some countries can be traced back to decolonization.

Health in Western Africa

The state of public health in western Africa is markedly worse than in northern Africa and developed countries. People live shorter lives and have less access to health care, and many die each year from circumstances related to poverty—such as malnutrition and limited access to clean water. In this chapter, we will examine the state of public health in the region and look in depth at some ways that widespread poverty can contribute to poor health.

Life Expectancy

Life expectancy in western Africa is low when compared to the rest of the world. The one exception is Cabo Verde, a small island nation in the Atlantic Ocean, where average life expectancy is seventy-four years old. On the mainland, this number is much lower. In Nigeria—the most populous country in the region and home to more than half the people in all of western Africa—average expectancy was just fifty-four years in 2015. This means that, on average, a child born today in Nigeria will die a shocking twenty-four years earlier than a child born today in the United States. A number of facts contribute to this disparity in life expectancy between western Africa (and sub-Saharan Africa in general) and developed countries. They include widespread malnutrition, high maternal and child mortality due to limited health care, and high levels of deadly infectious diseases like HIV/AIDS, tuberculosis, and malaria.

Malnutrition: A Preventable Killer

Malnutrition is a major public health concern across sub-Saharan Africa. Some 3.1 million deaths around the world each year are due to malnutrition—mostly in sub-Saharan Africa and parts of Asia. Malnutrition can be due to a number of reasons; the WHO identifies three: "People are malnourished if they are unable to utilize fully the food they eat, for example due to diarrhoea or other illnesses (secondary malnutrition), if they consume too many calories (overnutrition), or if their diet does not provide adequate calories and protein for growth and maintenance (undernutrition or protein-energy malnutrition)." In sub-Saharan Africa, all three of these types of malnutrition are pressing problems. While you might not think of obesity and diabetes when you think of health in Africa, they are in fact increasing rapidly. In the future, they will likely be the primary form of malnutrition (as they are now in developed countries).

The negative effects of malnutrition are most serious in children. Chronic malnutrition in early childhood leads to stunted growth. This in turn leads to a lifetime of negative consequences. Children with stunted growth do not reach their full physical or cognitive capabilities in life. Not only are they shorter than their peers who had access to nutritious food, they also suffer from impaired cognitive abilities for the rest of their lives. Malnourished children are also much more likely to die from common infections, like diarrheal diseases, because they are in poor health to begin with. For these reasons, many programs that fight malnutrition target young children. The cycle of poverty and malnutrition is easiest to break at an early age before the lifelong effects of stunted growth occur.

Clean Water

One thing we often take for granted in life is access to clean water. We need only to turn on the tap or go to nearby convenience store for safe, affordable water. But for more than a billion people around the world, clean drinking water is not accessible. This has a number of negative consequences when it comes to health. Contaminated drinking water can lead to a plethora of diseases, including diarrhea, typhoid, and cholera. It can also contain parasites that inflict great suffering. Huge strides have been made recently in expanding access to clean water. According to the WHO, in 1990 only 76 percent of people around the world had access to clean water. That number has increased to 91 percent as of 2015. But that means that 9 percent of the world's population is still forced to drink contaminated water on a regular basis. These people are often the most vulnerable, those living in poor or rural areas with little access to health care. As a result, hundreds of thousands of people die each year from unsafe drinking water—most of them children and most due to diarrheal diseases. We will take a more in-depth look at these diseases, one of the leading causes of child mortality, later in this chapter.

Maternal Mortality

The maternal mortality rate (MMR) is often given as a single number. For instance, the MMR of the United States in 2015 was 14. What this means is that for every 100,000 live births in the country, 14 women die from complications of pregnancy or childbirth. This number is quite low—it is rare for a woman in the United States to die from pregnancy or childbirth. But in many countries of the world the MMR is high. In Nigeria the MMR was 814 in 2015, or more than fifty times higher than it is the United States. In Sierra Leone (in western Africa) the MMR is even higher at 1,360. But in Ghana, another country in the region, the MMR is 319. While this is still above the world average of 216, it is far lower than in Nigeria or Sierra Leone. Limited access to health care before, during, and after birth is the reason that the MMR is so high in western Africa. Countries in the region are trying to change this, and some gains have been made in the past few decades, but there remains a great deal of progress to be made.

Infectious Diseases

The state of infectious diseases in western Africa is very different from that of northern Africa. HIV/AIDS and malaria, largely absent from northern Africa, are grave public health concerns for western Africa. More than three million people living in Nigeria suffer from HIV/AIDS—this is the second largest number of people in a single country with the disease, after South Africa. The rate of HIV/AIDS is also significant in the other countries of the region. Likewise, the incidence of malaria in western Africa is also very high. More than 90 percent of deaths from malaria around the world occur in sub-Saharan Africa, and western Africa is no exception to this. The disease occurs in every western African country and is a significant threat to public health.

Diarrheal Diseases

In developed countries, we think of diarrhea as an inconvenience, not as a life-threatening symptom of disease. But for billions of people around the world, diarrhea can result in death. For children under the age of five, it is the second leading cause of death (after malnutrition). More than 750,000 children die each year from diarrheal diseases, despite the fact that these diseases are easily managed and are not likely to be fatal with basic medical care.

Diarrheal diseases are caused by a number of different things. The most common causes are *E. coli* infection (a bacterial infection in the digestive system) and rotavirus (a type of virus that is common around the world). Most diarrheal diseases result from the ingestion of water contaminated with fecal matter. This is why access to clean drinking water is such an important issue for human health. When death results from diarrheal diseases, it is usually due to dehydration. Prolonged episodes of diarrhea cause a loss of water and electrolytes (like sodium and potassium) in the body. With time, this can cause severe dehydration and eventually death.

Diarrhea is relatively simple to treat. Drinking a solution of water and electrolytes (called an oral rehydration solution) is usually enough to prevent serious complications. This treatment is incredibly cheap, costing only a few cents. But it is still out of reach for many people around the world, especially in sub-Saharan Africa. Another effective treatment of diarrhea in children is zinc supplementation. Zinc is an essential mineral that is important for the health of cells in the human body. When children suffering from diarrhea take zinc, it decreases the severity and duration of their symptoms as well as making it less likely they will suffer from diarrhea in the near future. Like oral rehydration solution, zinc is a cheap, effective means of treating diarrhea and preventing further health complications.

Even when diarrheal diseases do not immediately cause death, they can compromise the health of children. Diarrhea is the leading cause of malnutrition in children—and malnutrition also makes diarrheal diseases more prevalent. This fact leads to a cycle wherein children who suffer from malnutrition develop

Oral rehydration salts are dissolved in water. Those suffering from diarrheal diseases drink the solution to prevent dehydration.

diarrheal disease, which in turn leads to severe malnutrition and further increased risk of diarrheal disease.

The best defense against diarrheal diseases is improved access to clean water and improved sanitation. Treatment for dehydration in affected individuals is also a key factor in decreasing mortality. In the future, vaccinations may play an important role in the fight against diarrheal diseases. There is a vaccine for the most common form of rotavirus, which is effective in preventing a large proportion of diarrheal disease. Its use varies from country to country, but it is not routine for all children in sub-Sahara Africa to receive it. In the future, this may change as the WHO continues to urge the governments of many countries to adopt national immunization programs.

Ebola Virus Disease

In 2013, the Ebola virus appeared in headlines around the world as an outbreak occurred in western Africa. Beginning in Guinea, it soon spread to the neighboring countries of Sierra Leone and Liberia. By the time the outbreak ended in 2016, more than ten thousand people had died from the disease. This recent outbreak was the most deadly and widespread outbreak of Ebola in history. Until 2013, confirmed cases of Ebola virus disease had claimed the lives of only 1,528 people since the virus was discovered, according to the Centers for Disease Control and Prevention (CDC). The actual number of fatalities from Ebola is likely much higher than these numbers of confirmed fatalities. People who did not know they had the disease or decided not to seek treatment may not be included in these figures.

The Ebola virus was first identified in 1972 in two separate outbreaks outside of western Africa. It gained international notoriety for its extremely high fatality rate: more than half of those who contract the virus die. At first,

The Ebola virus was initially transmitted to humans by bats.

the symptoms of Ebola virus disease are nondescript and include fever, tiredness, and headache. But later more serious symptoms such as vomiting and diarrhea arise. In some cases, bleeding occurs both internally and externally—usually from the nose and gums. (Although it is the most famous symptom of the disease, bleeding is actually relatively rare.) The majority of people die within six to sixteen days of showing symptoms of the virus. Death usually results from the failure of the circulatory system due to low blood pressure (from fluid loss), the failure of multiple organs, and shock. Those who survive often have long-term complications from the disease, such as vision loss and joint pain.

Ebola virus disease is treated with oral or intravenous (IV) fluids and the treatment of symptoms. While this does slightly increase the chance of survival, the fatality rate is still often above 50 percent. There is currently no treatment for

Smallpox: The Red Plague

Smallpox was an infectious disease that caused a rash that would turn into fluid-filled blisters and then sores. The disease was often fatal, and those lucky enough to survive usually had scars from the rash. Smallpox was endemic to Europe, Africa, and Asia for much of history and arrived in the Americas with European explorers. The smallpox vaccine, developed in 1796, was the first vaccine in the world. Edward Jenner discovered that smallpox could be prevented by exposing people to cowpox (a related disease). Before this discovery, there were crude attempts to prevent the transmission of smallpox. Variolation—the rubbing of smallpox scabs or pus into open wounds—was used by people in many parts of the world, including Africa and Europe. People who underwent variolation contracted a less serious form of the disease that then granted them immunity against smallpox in the future. Approximately 3 percent of people who underwent the procedure died. But variolation was still practiced because the mortality rate of smallpox was much higher: close to 30 percent.

Smallpox vaccination campaigns began throughout much of Africa as soon as European powers carved the continent into colonies at the end of the 1800s and beginning of the 1900s. Vaccination was often mandatory, although the delivery of the vaccine in remote areas with little infrastructure was problematic. Outbreaks of smallpox continued until most African countries achieved their independence during the 1950s and 1960s.

Smallpox was finally eradicated in 1977. Today, the virus exists only in laboratories. Smallpox was the first infectious disease to be eradicated, and it remains a symbol of what can be accomplished by a coordinated global campaign against a disease.

Ebola itself, but a number of treatments and two vaccines are currently being evaluated for future use.

Though there are often sensationalist media reports about Ebola becoming a global pandemic, these fears are often overblown. Ebola is extremely deadly but relatively hard to transmit. It requires direct contact with bodily fluids and cannot be spread through the air like the common cold or flu. This means it is unlikely to become an epidemic in countries with strong health care systems that can respond rapidly to an outbreak and monitor those exposed to the virus.

Conflict and Health: The Aftermath of War

In the first chapter, we looked at the toll that violence takes on people who are caught up in conflicts. But even after hostilities cease, the effects of war continue to linger. Both the combatants and civilians who lived through the conflict may bear psychological and physical scars. These leave a lasting impact on the lives of the population and stress the health care system of a country.

The psychological effect of witnessing violence firsthand can be devastating. The WHO report *Mental Health: New Understanding, New Hope* describes how wars and unrest can have widespread implications for mental health:

> Such situations take a heavy toll on the mental health of the people involved, most of whom live in developing countries, where capacity to take care of these problems is extremely limited. Between a third and half of all the affected persons suffer from mental distress. The most frequent diagnosis made is **post-traumatic stress disorder (PTSD)**,

often along with depressive or anxiety disorders. In addition, most individuals report psychological symptoms that do not amount to disorders. PTSD arises after a stressful event of an exceptionally threatening or catastrophic nature and is characterized by intrusive memories, avoidance of circumstances associated with the stressor, sleep disturbances, irritability and anger, lack of concentration and excessive vigilance.

You may have heard of PTSD before in the context of soldiers and veterans, but it can also affect civilians who witnessed a traumatic event in or outside of war. It can be a debilitating disorder, but it is treatable with therapy by a trained professional. Unfortunately, treatment for PTSD, depression, and anxiety disorders is often unavailable in developing countries, where major diseases sometimes take priority over mental health.

In addition to psychological trauma, victims of violence are sometimes left with permanent injuries. These can make life difficult and place a financial burden on the person who suffers from them, as well as on the health care system of a country. Injuries like amputations can lead to ongoing medical expenses as prosthetics need to be replaced. Other conditions that result from war, such as blindness, can also require ongoing medical treatment. These types of permanent injuries often strain the economy of a country; greater medical care is needed while at the same time people with disabilities may be unable to do the work they previously did.

The Sierra Leone civil war illustrates the massive impact that disabling injuries can have on an entire country. Between the years of 1991 and 2002 a civil war gripped the western African country of Sierra Leone. Rebel forces, supported by American-educated warlord and Liberian president Charles Taylor, committed heinous atrocities against the civilian population of Sierra Leone. They amputated the limbs (most often the hands), ears, noses, and lips of civilians who were suspected of supporting the government. The war left tens of thousands dead and thousands more disabled. The public health system was unable to treat this influx of amputees, especially when a war and political crisis gripped the country. **Nongovernmental organizations (NGOs)**, including national and international charities, attempted to provide basic health care to amputees, but they were not able to treat everyone. Additionally, most international charities gradually left after the conflict ended, despite the fact that amputees required continued health care services. Today, it is difficult for Sierra Leoneans with disabilities to receive adequate health care. This is a problem not only for the people themselves who suffer as a result, but also for the country, as it slows down its economic development.

While the widespread use of amputations as a weapon of terror makes the Sierra Leone civil war a stark example of the cost of war to the survivors, all wars leave scars on those who survive. The physical and psychological damage from war are a public health concern in all countries with a history of conflict. This damage burdens the health care system and economy and fundamentally alters the lives of survivors and their families.

Nigeria: Primary Health Care Reform

Nigeria is the most populous country in Africa: one in six Africans is Nigerian, and the country is home to more than five hundred different languages. This presents a number of challenges for the country's health care sector. Services need to

Clinics in rural areas are an essential way of making health care accessible in many parts of Africa.

be provided across a large country to a huge number of people who speak different languages. In September 2015, Nigerian health care advocates Muhammed M. Lecky and Tunde Segun wrote, "poor health outcomes persist throughout the country." Average life expectancy is low, and many die from preventable causes of death such as complications of childbirth and malnutrition.

Primary health care (PHC) receives a great deal of attention in writings about improving health care in developing countries. The WHO outlined and promoted PHC in the Declaration of Alma-Ata in 1978. According to this declaration, PHP is:

> essential health care based on practical, scientifically sound and socially acceptable methods and technology made universally accessible to individuals and families in the community through their full participation and at a cost that the community and country can afford to maintain at every stage of their development in the spirit of self-reliance and self-determination.

In other words, the goal of PHC is that health care is available to everyone no matter their wealth. Health care should be based on the needs and expectations of the communities that access it. In countries with weak health care systems, an effective PHC system is especially important: if it is divorced from communities, difficult to navigate, expensive, or seen as ineffective people may not seek out medical care in the future. The longer people wait to seek treatment for diseases like malaria and HIV/AIDS, the more expensive the treatment and the worse the **prognosis** (or medical outlook).

Nigerian health care advocates Lecky and Segun report that health care in Nigeria is set to improve in the future because of recent improvements in PHC in the country. They write:

> We are optimistic because, first, we are pleased by early evidence that Nigeria's Primary Health Care Under One Roof (PHCUOR) policies seem to be succeeding. Instituted in 2011 to address intractable stewardship and governance problems facing Nigeria's health care delivery system, the policies were designed to facilitate better management of resources by health care managers, increase patient confidence in and utilization of services, increase efficiency and coordination of health services, and reduce fragmentation.

It remains to be seen how effective PHCUOR will be in the future, but it is a step in the right direction for health care in Nigeria.

Central Africa is home to large tracts of rain forest.

3 | Central Africa

There are nine countries in central Africa. All of them except for the small island nation of São Tomé and Príncipe and the oil-rich country of Gabon have high levels of poverty. In fact, the two poorest countries in the world (based on their per capita GDP) are both in central Africa: the Central African Republic and Burundi. Due to this fact, we will examine the complex relationship between poverty and health in this chapter.

But there is more to central Africa than just poverty. The people of the region have many rich cultural traditions. The region contains almost all of Africa's tropical rain forests, although much of the region is covered in grassland. The climate is mostly tropical with the exception of the Central African Republic (part of which is located in the Sahara Desert). This means that neglected tropical diseases are common to the region—especially when compared to northern or southern Africa, which do not have tropical climates.

Health in Central Africa

The state of health in central Africa is among the worst in the world. High levels of poverty and malnutrition, combined with poor vaccination coverage, mean that maternal and infant mortality are high, life expectancy is low, and preventable

Albert Schweitzer's Hospital

The impact of colonization on health in Africa was not universally negative. While most hospitals established by colonial powers on the continent catered to the needs of white Europeans, there were some exceptions. One of the most famous is the Albert Schweitzer Hospital, located in the central African country of Gabon. The hospital was founded in 1913 by Albert Schweitzer, a French-German theologian and physician. According to journalist David Baron, "His goal was to alleviate suffering. He said he wanted to

The grounds of the Albert Schweitzer Hospital

atone for the sins white Europeans had committed against black Africans." The hospital fulfilled this mission under Schweitzer's direction until his death in 1965. It offered quality health care that was usually paid for by charity. Schweitzer received a Nobel Peace Prize for his life's work, including his operation of the hospital, in 1952. Since Schweitzer's death, the hospital has continued to operate. As in its early history, the hospital was run primarily by European administrators and on charitable contributions raised from Europe. But that recently changed in 2012. After years of conflict between European and Gabonese board members, a Gabonese hospital director was elected. Funds were also sought from the government of Gabon rather than charity abroad. According to David Baron, "The Albert Schweitzer Hospital still faces huge obstacles: A million-dollar budget deficit, antiquated facilities, a rising burden of HIV and tuberculosis. But for the first time since the hospital was founded nearly 100 years ago, an African is in charge."

deaths claim many lives each year. However, the opportunity for improving public health is great. A number of charities, NGOs, and national governments are attempting to curb these public health concerns and help people in the region live longer, healthier lives.

Maternal Mortality

The lifetime risk of maternal death is another way that the risk of dying from complications of pregnancy or childbirth is measured. It is the chance that a fifteen-year-old female will die as a result of pregnancy or childbirth, assuming the birth rate and MMR do not change. The lifetime risk of maternal death in the United States is just one in thirty-eight thousand. Compare this to one in eighteen in the central African country of Chad. The central African country with the lowest lifetime risk of maternal death is the small island nation of São Tomé and Príncipe at one in one hundred forty. Most countries in central Africa (and sub-Saharan Africa as a whole) fall closer to the bottom of this range. These figures mean hundreds of women die each day in Africa from complications of pregnancy or childbirth.

Infant Mortality

Children across central Africa have between a 4 and 9 percent chance of dying before their first birthday—depending on the country they are born in. In developed countries like the United States and Canada this falls to 0.5 percent. This exceptionally high infant mortality rate in central Africa is due to a number of factors: chief among them is limited access to health care and high rates of malnutrition. But one important factor we have not discussed is vaccines.

Vaccines (and Measles)

Vaccines are an important part of global efforts to reduce child mortality. They are also a cost-effective and scientifically proven way to do so. This makes vaccination campaigns a popular endeavor for charities like the Bill and Melinda Gates Foundation. While the cost of the recommended package of vaccines for a child is less than $40, this is a substantial amount of money for the hundreds of millions of Africans who live on less than $1.90 a day. The fact that many vaccines must be refrigerated also complicates their distribution to remote locations. As a result of the high price and logistical difficulties in administering vaccines, 1.5 million children die each year from vaccine-preventable diseases around the world.

There are a number of vaccine-preventable diseases responsible for this great number of fatalities. They include diphtheria (or whooping cough—a bacterial respiratory infection), hepatitis B (a viral disease that affects the liver), and polio (a viral infection of the central nervous system). These, and many other vaccine-preventable diseases, can cause death or disability in the unvaccinated. The region of the world with the worst vaccination coverage is sub-Saharan Africa. Central Africa in particular suffers from numerous outbreaks of **measles**—one of the most common vaccine-preventable diseases.

Measles is a viral respiratory infection that seriously compromises the immune system of those who suffer from it. It can lead to lifelong health complications such as brain damage and blindness in those who survive. Though it is rarely fatal in the developed world, it can kill up to 40 percent of those infected in situations where people live in cramped, unsanitary conditions, such as refugee camps.

A measles outbreak in the Democratic Republic of the Congo in 2015 resulted in nearly 40,000 cases of the disease, mostly among children between the ages of one and five. More than 450 people died from the disease—almost all of them children. These figures come from the humanitarian organization Doctors Without Borders, an international NGO that delivers medical care to those in need. (This group is also commonly referred to as MSF based on its French name: Médecins Sans Frontières.) In response to this measles outbreak in the Democratic Republic of the Congo, Doctors Without Borders vaccinated hundreds of thousands of children and treated thousands more who had developed measles. The actions of NGOs such as Doctors Without Borders save thousands of lives when outbreaks occur in developing and war-torn nations. These humanitarian NGOs and international organizations are also often the ones who provide free vaccines to people living in poverty in remote areas and conflict zones.

One benefit of high vaccination coverage is an effect called "herd protection" or "herd immunity." This refers to the fact that when a significant enough portion of a population is vaccinated against a disease, fewer people who are *not* vaccinated are infected. This typically occurs when approximately 80 percent or more of a population is vaccinated. At this point, even those who do not receive the vaccine are less likely to get infected because the disease becomes rare in the population. In some cases, this can even lead to the eradication of a disease in a population. According to the WHO, in one notable case, "Hib vaccine coverage of less than 70% in the Gambia was sufficient to eliminate Hib disease [a type of bacterial infection]." Herd immunity can be especially important when vaccines are not safe for infants. If all—or most—adults receive the vaccine, infants are protected because there is no one to expose them to the disease.

Infectious Disease

Infectious diseases are a major public health concern in central Africa. HIV/AIDS, tuberculosis, and malaria present a grave threat to public health in the region, as they do throughout sub-Saharan Africa. Depending on the country, between 1 and 5 percent of the population is living with HIV/AIDS. The mortality rate of these diseases, as well as other infectious diseases, is increased by widespread malnutrition and limited vaccinations. Many neglected tropical diseases are also endemic to the region due to its tropical climate and limited government spending to combat them. In addition to these diseases that we have discussed, lower respiratory tract infections also kill many people in the region, often as a result of preventable environmental factors.

Lower Respiratory Tract Infections

The lower respiratory tract is made up of the lungs, the bronchial tubes (the tubes that bring air to the lungs), and the trachea (or windpipe). While public health professionals often group all lower respiratory tract infections together, you have probably heard of the most common under their medical names: pneumonia (infection of the lungs) and bronchitis (infection of the bronchial tubes). Pneumonia and bronchitis can result from a number of causes, including viruses, bacteria, and fungi.

Lower respiratory tract infections are treatable. The exact treatment depends on the cause: antibiotics are used to combat bacterial infections while other drugs may be used for viral and fungal infections. In people who are otherwise healthy, these infections are rarely fatal. But due to factors such as malnutrition and household air pollution, lower respiratory tract infections kill more than a million people each year in sub-Saharan Africa. Most of these deaths are preventable. This makes lower respiratory tract infections the second leading cause of death in Africa after AIDS.

Nearly half of lower respiratory tract infections in Africa result from household air pollution. The greatest contributor to household air pollution is burning solid fuel to cook. Another source of household air pollution is second-hand tobacco smoke, though this is a larger concern in developed nations. A report by the World Bank sums up the relationship between cooking indoors and human health:

> Reliance on solid-fuel cooking in Sub-Saharan Africa (SSA) is a large and growing problem.

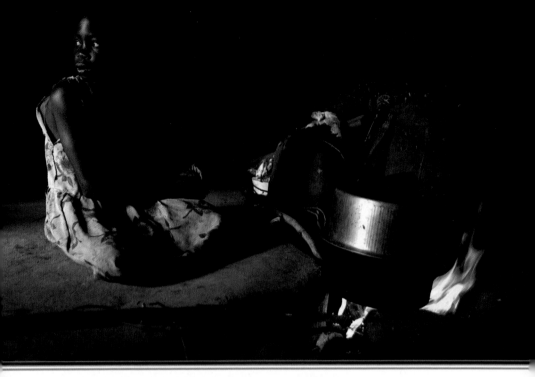

Cooking indoors with solid fuel is a serious health risk.

More than 700 million Africans (82%) use solid fuels, such as wood, charcoal, dung, crop waste, and coal, for their primary cooking needs—a number that will reach 850–900 million by the end of the decade. This high level of solid-fuel use, combined with household reliance on inefficient and unsafe traditional cookstoves, constitutes a first-order public health crisis: household air pollution (HAP) from solid-fuel cooking emissions kills nearly 600,000 Africans annually and is now recognized as the second-largest health risk factor in terms of death and disability in the region.

In addition to the lower respiratory tract infections we have discussed, household air pollution can also cause lung cancer, heart disease, and low birth rate, among other health problems.

The problem of burning solid fuels indoors is difficult to solve. The root of the problem is poverty. Solid fuels such as wood and dung are often free, while clean fuels like electricity and liquefied petroleum gas are relatively expensive. Additionally, using electricity or gas requires a very large upfront cost for the stove itself. In many areas, electricity and gas are themselves hard to come by, even if one does have the money and desire to cook with them. Power shortages are common across Africa, and access to gas is often lacking. People are also often unaware of the dangers of burning solid fuel indoors and are reluctant to give up traditional cooking methods when the harm from household air pollution is not visible. Until clean cooking equipment is affordable and available to everyone in Africa, the health problems related to burning solid fuels indoors will continue to persist.

Rabies

Rabies is considered a neglected tropical disease by the WHO. Even though it is present on all continents except Antarctica, it is primarily a public health concern in Africa and Asia, where it kills tens of thousands of people every year. By comparison, less than five people a year generally die from rabies in the United States. While a vaccine does exist that prevents transmission of the disease, it is generally not recommended for people unless they are at high risk for developing the disease, for instance if they are traveling through remote areas where rabies is endemic or work with the virus in a lab. Instead, the WHO focuses on vaccinating dogs, the most common transmitter of the disease to humans.

Rabies in an infectious viral disease. The virus is transmitted through the bite or scratch of an infected animal. While the disease can affect all mammals, it is most commonly transmitted to people through a dog bite. Once bitten, there is a one- to three-month incubation period. During this time, there are no symptoms of rabies but the virus is spreading through the body. After the incubation period, symptoms appear. At this stage, death is virtually inevitable within ten days. However, the prognosis is good if treatment is given after exposure to the virus but before symptoms occur.

Post-exposure **prophylaxis** (or treatment to prevent a disease) is the only way to make survival likely. If treatment occurs within ten days of exposure to the virus, the infection can be prevented and no symptoms of the disease will occur. Prophylaxis involves three steps: the cleaning of the wound

Most cases of rabies in humans result from stray dogs biting children.

itself to kill any of the virus that is still at the site, the injection of the rabies vaccine four times over the course of two weeks, and the administration of the rabies immunoglobulin (or antibody) in severe cases.

Only a handful of people have survived rabies without post-exposure prophylaxis or previous vaccination. People used to think the disease was always fatal, but that changed in 2004 when an American girl was successfully treated after becoming infected with rabies. Her doctors induced a coma, preventing the disease from damaging her brain while giving her immune system time to fight the disease. After spending seven days in a coma, she was brought out of it—spending more than thirty days in the hospital while she recovered. Her course of treatment became known as the Milwaukee Protocol, and it has been used on a number of patients since 2004. But the survival rate is still less than 10 percent, and the treatment itself costs hundreds of thousands of dollars. This makes it too expensive in poorer regions of the world where rabies is more common.

The disease itself can take two forms in humans: furious rabies or paralytic rabies. Furious rabies is characterized by agitation, hyperactivity, and hydrophobia (fear of water). Paralytic rabies is characterized by paralysis spreading from the site of the bite or scratch followed by coma. Death from both types results from cardiac arrest or paralysis of the respiratory system.

Conflict and Health: The Indirect Deaths of War

During a conflict, there are both direct deaths (due to violence) and **indirect deaths** (consequences of the conflict but not due to violence). We looked at direct deaths in chapter one: these are usually the result of small arms in modern wars. But indirect deaths actually make up the majority of deaths due to conflict. Indirect deaths result from causes we have looked at—often malnutrition, a lack of access to health care, disrupted vaccinations, and unsafe drinking water all play a role. Deaths due to these factors are classified as indirect deaths due to conflict when it is the conflict that leads to these situations. As you may have guessed, it can be difficult to gather precise data on the exact number of indirect deaths a conflict causes. But it is possible to arrive at an estimate by looking at the mortality rate of a region before a conflict and then calculating the mortality rate during a conflict. That difference is the number of deaths due to the conflict. Once you subtract the number of direct deaths, only the indirect deaths remain. This number is almost always higher than the direct deaths—often there are many times more indirect deaths than direct deaths.

Even in countries that routinely suffer from problems like malnutrition and a lack of health care, conflict can exacerbate these issues and cause many more deaths. During times of war, there is often widespread hunger as farmers are forced to flee their land, shipments of food cannot be transported to cities, and economies collapse. People may be forced to flee into the countryside where there is no clean water or shelter. Hospitals are often shut down as they are targeted by violence and health care workers flee the country. Sometimes people are forced into unsanitary refugee camps where diseases decimate a malnourished population. All of these circumstances can lead to indirect deaths. In many ways, the threat of violence often causes more deaths than violence itself as people are forced to flee their homes.

The Second Congo War provides an example of the toll that indirect deaths can take on a population. The war began in the DRC in 1998, but it soon involved countries across the continent. Most of the fighting took place in the DRC, and as a result millions were forced to flee their homes to live in the wilderness or in refugee camps. By the time the war ended in 2002, the number of indirect deaths had reached unprecedented levels for recent history. It remains the deadliest conflict since World War II. According to the Geneva Declaration on Armed Violence and Development, indirect deaths are staggering in contemporary Africa:

> In almost all contemporary conflicts, the number of indirect victims of armed violence is many times larger than the number of battle deaths. The International Rescue Committee's series of mortality surveys in the Democratic Republic of the Congo (DRC) found that 5.4 million excess deaths occurred between August 1998 and April 2007, with 2.1 million occurring since the formal end of war in 2002 (Coghlan et al., 2008). Of these 5.4 million excess deaths since 1998, fewer than ten per cent died "directly" or violently. Nearly all deaths (90 per cent)—approximately 4.8 million people—were indirect and caused mainly by preventable infectious diseases, malnutrition, and neonatal- and pregnancy-related conditions that emerged in the resource-poor post-conflict environment.

As we can see, indirect deaths are often the deadliest part of a conflict. Many more civilians die far from home in crowded refugee camps than soldiers die on the battlefield.

Sleeping Sickness

Sleeping sickness (or African trypanosomiasis) is a parasitic disease that is almost always fatal. Categorized as a neglected tropical disease, it is spread by the tsetse fly, which carries a species of parasitic **protozoa** from host to host. Initial symptoms include fever and headaches. After the disease infects the central nervous systems, symptoms progress to confusion, lethargy, tremor, disturbances to the sleep cycle (for which the disease is named), and eventually coma and death.

Sleeping sickness was well known to colonial officials in Africa. It presented a threat to the profitability of the African colonies because it kills cattle as well as people. In 1903, David Bruce, a Scottish doctor, identified the specific protozoa that causes sleeping sickness and confirmed that the tsetse fly is the vector of the disease. With this knowledge, colonial administrations began to wage a war against the disease. According to ecologist Ian Scoones:

> Colonial authorities ordered large scale bush clearance and wildlife extermination programmes. These were major efforts, involving armies of people, clearing bush with machetes and trapping and shooting wildlife. The scale was phenomenal. For example around 750,000 animals were shot in Zimbabwe between 1932 and when the game destruction policy was stopped in 1961.

Additionally, chemicals like DDT—a now banned insecticide—were sprayed across huge areas of Africa to kill the tsetse fly. These attempts to eradicate the disease did not succeed. Eventually, they were discontinued as people began to question the environmental impact of these practices. Today, the disease still exists, although treatments are available. Each year, there are approximately ten thousand cases of sleeping sickness in Africa, mostly in the DRC.

The Democratic Republic of the Congo: Extreme Poverty and Health

The Democratic Republic of the Congo (DRC) is the most populous country in central Africa. It is also the most populous country in the world where more than 75 percent of the population lives in **extreme poverty**. The World Bank defines extreme poverty as living on less than $1.90 a day—an impossibly small sum to support a healthy life with shelter, food, and medicine. As of 2012 (when the most recent data was gathered), 896 million people around the world lived in extreme poverty. A disproportionate number (388.7 million) lived in sub-Saharan Africa. This means that more than 40 percent of people living in extreme poverty are in sub-Saharan Africa, despite the fact that only 14 percent of the world's population lives there. Put another way, 42.6 percent of the population of sub-Saharan Africa lives in extreme poverty. This has a huge effect on the health of the region.

Poverty and health are closely related. The principal causes of poor health—malnutrition and limited access to clean water, vaccines, and health care—all usually stem from poverty. Additionally, poor health can cause poverty or vice versa. A cycle of poverty and poor health is often discussed in reports about health in developing countries. A report by the Organization for Economic Co-operation and Development describes the relationship between poverty and health in the following way:

> The poor suffer worse health and die younger. They have higher than average child and maternal mortality, higher levels of disease, more limited access to health care and social protection. And gender inequality disadvantages further the health of poor women and girls. For poor people especially, health is also a crucially important economic asset. Their livelihoods depend on it. When a poor or socially vulnerable person becomes ill or injured, the entire household can become trapped in a downward spiral of lost income and high health care costs. The cascading effects may include diverting time from generating an income or from schooling to care for the sick; they may also force the sale of assets required for livelihoods. Poor people are more vulnerable to this downward spiral as they are more prone to disease and have more limited access to health care and social insurance.

Poverty takes a terrible toll on public health in the DRC—especially for children. More than 40 percent of children under the age of five suffer from stunted growth.

One in eight children die before their fifth birthday. In circumstances like this, any **health shock** (a term for an unforeseen illness) can quickly lead to extreme poverty and an inability to pay for medical care. Most people in the DRC (and many other developing nations) must pay for medical care with **out-of-pocket health payments**. (This is not the case in some countries like Tunisia, the United States, or Canada, where most people's health care costs are covered by health insurance companies or the government.) Out-of-pocket health payments can bankrupt families. In practice, they also often mean that people do not seek medical care for illnesses that do not seem too serious: the cost of going to a clinic and buying medicine is too great to justify. This can have dire consequences as illnesses often become more difficult and expensive to treat the longer one waits.

Given these facts, it is no surprise that countries with high levels of extreme poverty tend to suffer when it comes to public health. The DRC is an example of a country where extreme poverty has resulted in some of the worst health outcomes in the world, although NGOs are also working in the country to combat the ill effects of poverty on health. There are some exceptions to this link between poverty and poor public health, and we will look at one (the small east African country of Rwanda) in the next chapter.

Hills and volcanoes are typical features of some parts of eastern Africa.

4 Eastern Africa

Eastern Africa is made up of fourteen countries. Kenya and Ethiopia are the economic powerhouses of the region, followed by Tanzania. But the GDP per capita is quite low in every country in eastern Africa with the exception of the rich islands of the Seychelles and Mauritius. However, only a tiny fraction of the region's population resides in these island nations where the economy is largely driven by tourism. Eastern Africa spans a large area of Africa north to south, and this leads to some important cultural differences. The countries at the northernmost reaches of the region—Sudan and Somalia—are Muslim majority, while Christianity is the dominant religion farther south. The security situation in the region is also quite varied; many states are stable but conflicts rage in others. Somalia has been the site of near constant conflict since the ongoing Somali civil war began in 1991, and South Sudan, the world's newest state, which gained its independence in 2011, is also engaged in an ongoing civil war between rival political factions.

Health in Eastern Africa

Public health in eastern Africa is similar to rest of sub-Saharan Africa. Child and maternal mortality—

preventable causes of death—take a heavy toll on the people of the region. Malnutrition exists to varying degrees in the diverse countries of the region, lowering average life expectancy and raising child mortality rates. Access to health care is limited for many people due to poverty and living in rural areas. But like most of Africa, there have been recent improvements in public health that are a cause for optimism.

Polio and African Defenders of Public Health

Oftentimes books about health in developing nations look primarily at UN agencies, international NGOs, and famous scientists. But the people on the front lines of the fight against disease, malnutrition, and death are often people from the affected area. Ali Maow Maalin was one Somalian man who spent years fighting infectious disease in his native country. He is also a notable figure in the history of health because he was the last person in the world to contract smallpox (outside of a laboratory).

In 1977, Maalin was working as a cook at a hospital in Somalia. Although all hospital staff were required to be vaccinated against smallpox, he managed to avoid the vaccine because he was afraid the shot would hurt. He later came down with smallpox but survived the disease. After his illness, he committed himself to fighting another infectious disease, polio, in his home country. (Polio is one of the infectious diseases most likely to be eradicated in the future.) He volunteered to go door-to-door to immunize children in the then war-torn country. He also helped convince militia leaders and local parents that the vaccine was safe by relating his own personal experience

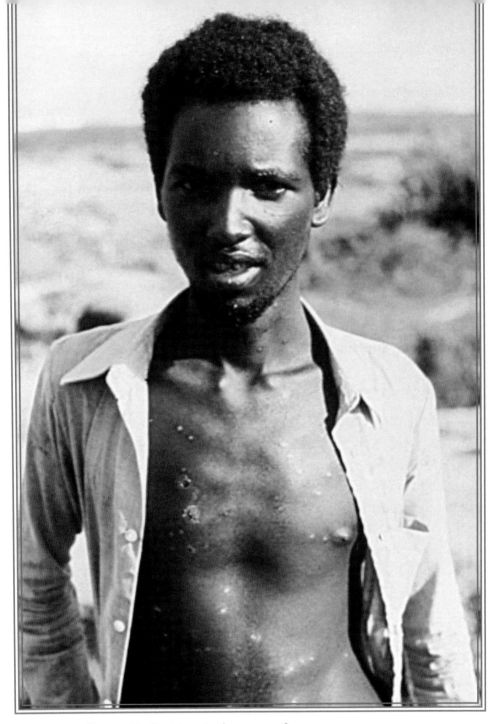

Ali Maow Maalin at twenty-three years of age

with smallpox. According to the *Boston Globe*, Maalin described this aspect of his work by saying, "Now when I meet parents who refuse to give their children the polio vaccine, I tell them my story. I tell them how important these vaccines are. I tell them not to do something foolish like me."

Between 1977 and 2013, Maalin volunteered for a number of polio immunization campaigns. During the last one, he developed a fever while volunteering. It turned out to be malaria, and he died days later from complications. Maalin was just one of the many local people who dedicated his life to improving health in his home country. He ultimately died due to his efforts, but thanks to his work and the work of others like him polio is no longer endemic to Somalia.

Infectious Disease

All of the most deadly diseases of the continent exist throughout eastern Africa: malaria, tuberculosis, HIV/AIDS, diarrheal diseases, and respiratory infections. They weigh heavily on public health in the region and cause numerous deaths. This chapter, we will take a closer look at malaria—one of the most famous and feared infectious diseases endemic to Africa—as well as dengue fever. Dengue fever is a disease that is getting increasing media coverage for large outbreaks in Asia and Latin America, but it also troubles Africa.

Malaria

As we saw in chapter one, malaria used to be endemic to most of the world: it has existed in every continent except Antarctica. But it has been eradicated in many

India: The Pharmacy of the Developing World

India is often called the pharmacy of the developing world because of the number of pharmaceuticals it sells. This is partially because India sells medicines at much lower prices than other countries due to its patent laws. When a company first discovers (or slightly alters) a drug, the company has exclusive rights to sell the medication for twenty years. This is so that it can recoup the cost of research and development of the new medication. But this also leads to prices that are out of reach for people in developing countries. However, India makes it more difficult for pharmaceutical companies to continuously patent the same medication by making small changes in formulation in a bid to increase profits. This has lowered the prices for medication in the developing world and has proved invaluable in the fight against HIV/AIDS in Africa and against other diseases. Doctors Without Borders describes the situation in the following way:

> India's law sets the bar higher for what deserves a patent than other countries, filtering out patent applications that cover simple changes to existing pharmaceutical products, in the interest of public health. This has allowed the robust **generic** competition to continue that has, for example, resulted in the price of a basic HIV treatment combination dropping by 99 percent

over the course of a decade, from over US$10,000 to around $100.

However, there has been recent pressure on the government of India from pharmaceutical companies and the United States (where most of the companies are based) to change its laws to benefit pharmaceutical companies and drive up the cost of medication. These changes are opposed by humanitarian organizations like Doctors Without Borders and governments of developing countries (especially South Africa). They argue that higher prices will put millions of lives in danger.

regions, including some parts of Africa. In Africa, it is now restricted to a wide band that stretches across the continent around the equator: it is no longer endemic to most of northern Africa and the southern tip of Africa. (Malaria is also endemic to parts of Asia and the Americas near the equator).

Malaria is a vector-borne infectious disease. It is caused by five species of parasitic protozoa that belong to the genus *Plasmodium*. The most deadly species, *Plasmodium falciparum*, resides in sub-Saharan Africa, and this is the region where 90 percent of deaths from malaria occur. The parasites are spread by some species of *Anopheles* mosquito. (Not all mosquitoes are capable of transmitting malaria.) The life cycle of these parasites is

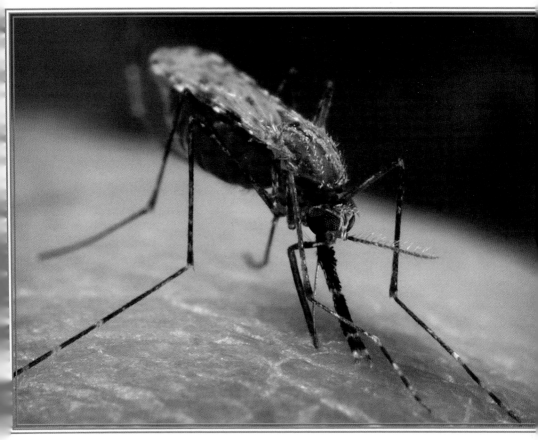

Only certain types of mosquitoes transmit malaria.

quite complex and takes place in both a human host and an insect host. The parasite takes a number of different forms and lives in a variety of places within the body. When an infected mosquito bites a human, the parasites are transmitted from the salivary glands of the mosquito to the blood stream of the human. The parasites then make their way to the liver of the human before changing their structure and once again reentering the blood stream to infect red blood cells. Then, when the human host is again bitten by a mosquito capable of carrying malaria, the parasites enter that mosquito, reproduce in the mosquito's digestive system, and return to the salivary glands to begin the cycle again.

Symptoms of malaria, including fever, fatigue, headache, vomiting, and chills usually occur between one and three weeks after being bitten by an infected mosquito. If the disease is not immediately treated at this stage, there is a chance that severe malaria will develop. Symptoms of severe malaria are quite diverse but universally serious. A report by the WHO states that the following symptoms can appear individually or in various combinations:

- Impaired consciousness (including unrousable coma);
- Prostration, i.e. generalized weakness so that the patient is unable to sit, stand or walk without assistance;
- Multiple convulsions: more than two episodes within 24h;
- Acute kidney injury;
- Clinical jaundice plus evidence of other vital organ dysfunction; and
- Abnormal bleeding.

Severe malaria is more common in young children and those living with AIDS. It is also more likely to result in death in these groups. Malaria kills more than half a million people a year in sub-Saharan Africa, making it the fourth leading cause of death in the region and the second most common cause of death in children under the age of five. As we have seen in previous chapters, malnutrition is often a contributing factor in many of these deaths.

There is currently no licensed vaccine for malaria. This means that the fight against malaria revolves around the fact that it is a vector-borne disease, and the most cost-effective means of combating malaria is the use of insecticide-treated mosquito nets (ITNs). People sleep inside of these nets during the night—when mosquito bites are most common. ITNs not only physically prevent the mosquito from biting a sleeping person, the insecticide they are coated with also kills mosquitos. ITNs have been shown to decrease the occurrence of malaria by approximately 50 percent in those who use them. This is a significant accomplishment, but the use of ITNs is problematic. Many nets need to be retreated with insecticide every six to twelve months (although some now last three years). Retreating the nets can present a problem for many people who lack resources or the knowledge of how to do this.

In addition to ITNs, indoor residual spraying (IRS) is another effective means of vector control. During IRS, the interior walls and surfaces of a house are covered with insecticide. When mosquitos rest on these surfaces, the insecticide kills them. However, neither ITNs nor IRS prevents all cases of malaria in a home or community.

Another means of malaria prevention that does not focus on vector control is chemoprevention. A number of antimalarial drugs prevent malaria from developing even when one is bitten by an infected mosquito. The WHO does not advise that everyone in regions where malaria is endemic take these drugs, though they are a powerful tool in the fight against malaria. Instead, the WHO recommends that only some vulnerable groups of people take these medications to prevent malaria. In particular, chemoprevention can help protect pregnant women and young children in regions where malaria is seasonal and not a year-round concern. (This includes much of the Sahel region on the outskirts of the Sahara Desert: malaria is most common during the rainy season there.)

Sadly, for more than two hundred million people a year these preventative measures fail. Treatment is available when this happens. For *P. falciparum* malaria (the most common in Africa), something called artemisinin-based combination therapy is recommended for treatment. A combination of drugs is used to both eliminate the parasites and decrease the chance that drug-resistant malaria develops from treatment. The prognosis for those suffering from malaria is quite good with treatment. However, once the disease has progressed to severe malaria the outlook is not as bright. This can be problematic in areas with limited access to health care. The initial symptoms of malaria, like fever, are often not noteworthy. By the time symptoms become serious, severe malaria may have developed and the prognosis is especially poor for vulnerable groups like children and pregnant women. If health care is expensive, this poses a further problem. Families must decide whether to pay a doctor to check for malaria when a minor fever arises. It is likely that the fever is not serious, but if it is malaria and they choose to wait, it may be too late.

Dengue Fever

Dengue fever is a neglected tropical disease that is endemic in the Americas, Asia, and Africa. It, like malaria, is spread by mosquitoes. But unlike malaria, dengue is a viral infection. The incidence of dengue infections has increased rapidly in recent years. In 2015, there were

A mosquito net protects those sleeping inside from diseases like malaria.

major outbreaks in the Philippines, Malaysia, and Brazil. There was even a small outbreak in Hawaii with more than a hundred people coming down with the disease. The number of cases in Africa is difficult to measure for a number of reasons: African countries do not officially report dengue infections to the WHO, and furthermore experts suspect that most cases of dengue are mistakenly believed to be malaria in Africa. Nevertheless, there is evidence that dengue outbreaks are becoming more common and occurring on a larger scale in Africa than ever before. In the future, the occurrence of dengue is expected to increase around the globe.

Dengue can only be transmitted by a limited number of species of mosquito. After being bitten by an infected mosquito, there is an incubation period of four to ten days when no symptoms occur. Once this period ends, typical symptoms include an extremely high fever (40°C/104°F), "severe headache, pain behind the eyes, muscle and joint pains, nausea, vomiting, swollen glands or rash," according to the WHO. Usually, one recovers from dengue fever in two to seven days without medical intervention. There is no antiviral treatment for dengue fever. However, in some cases, intensive treatment is required to ensure adequate hydration when complications such as bleeding and organ impairment arise. This is known as severe dengue, and it is fatal in one in five cases without medical intervention. With medical care, it is only fatal in one in a hundred cases.

As with malaria, the primary method of controlling dengue fever is vector control. Numerous methods are used to reduce mosquito populations. Since mosquitoes breed in standing water, reducing the amount of standing water is a

People living in refugee camps are often exposed to many health risks.

priority. The WHO outlines the following components of effective vector control:

- Preventing mosquitoes from accessing egg-laying habitats by environmental management and modification;

- Disposing of solid waste properly and removing artificial man-made habitats;

- Covering, emptying and cleaning of domestic water storage containers on a weekly basis;

- Applying appropriate insecticides to water storage outdoor containers

Recently, a dengue fever vaccine, Dengvaxia, has been licensed in four countries: Mexico, the Philippines, Brazil, and El Salvador. In April of 2016, the WHO officially endorsed the vaccine. While the vaccine does not always prevent infections of dengue fever, it greatly reduces the likelihood of severe complications. It is also especially effective in people who have previously been infected with dengue fever. This is a benefit because previous infection is a significant risk factor for severe dengue. Whether this new vaccine will be affordable or widely implemented remains to be seen, but it could be the beginning of a new chapter in the fight against dengue fever around the world.

Conflict and Health: Refugee Camps

Conflict often uproots people from their homes. This happens for a variety of reasons. Often, they fear for their lives when bombs fall nearby or fighting is raging in the streets outside. Sometimes, they flee to avoid being forced to fight in the conflict by armed groups. Still other times, the security situations makes it impossible to live in an area when water, electricity, and food shipments are cut off. For many people who flee conflict, their only option is to live in a refugee camp (outside their home country)

The Jigger Flea

With the arrival of European explorers and colonists in the New World, a wave of new diseases swept across the continent and decimated the indigenous people. Some scholars estimate that 80 to 90 percent of the population of North America died in the ensuing years. But some diseases also made their way from the New World to Africa. One such disease is tungiasis. Caused by a kind of flea, *Tunga penetrans* (or jigger flea), tungiasis is a skin disease that occurs when the flea burrows into the flesh of a person (usually in the hands or feet). The presence of the flea causes pain, swelling, inflammation, and itching. A lesion appears on the surface of the skin with a black dot in the center (which is actually the back part of the flea). After four to six weeks, the flea dies and the body repairs itself, although complications such as gangrene and tetanus sometimes occur. Tungiasis itself is not deadly, but complications sometimes are.

Members of Christopher Columbus's crew were the first Europeans to suffer from tungiasis. But the disease was well-known to indigenous Americans at that time. Pieces of pottery from the Incan civilization in South America depict a man with holes in his feet. The jigger flea was eventually brought from the New World to Africa on European ships, and it then spread across much of the continent. Today, many people in sub-Saharan Africa (especially in rural communities) suffer from tungiasis. The disease is prevalent in poor communities where shoes are not always available and floors are sometimes dirt (where the flea lives at the beginning of its life cycle).

or a camp for **internally displaced people** (inside their home country). According to the UN definition, a person is only a refugee if they leave their home country. If they flee their home but remain in their home country they are an internally displaced person (IDP). But the distinction between the two often makes little practical difference: conditions in refugee camps and camps for internally displaced people are similar.

Recently, the Syria refugee crisis has grabbed headlines around the world. The civil war there has forced millions to leave their homes and become refugees or IDPs. The ongoing conflicts in Afghanistan and Iraq have likewise resulted in large numbers of refugees and IDPs in those countries. As a result, the Middle East and North Africa are the regions with the largest number of IDPs, but this is closely followed by sub-Saharan Africa. Similarly, Syria and Afghanistan are the two countries with the largest number of refugees, but the next five countries (Somalia, Sudan, South Sudan, the DRC, and the Central African Republic) are all in Africa.

In fact, the largest refugee camp in the world is not in the Middle East: it is in the east African nation of Kenya. Three hundred thousand Somali refugees live in refugee camps in the Kenyan town of Dadaab. They are refugees of decades of conflict in Somalia and a recent famine in 2011. Like most camps for displaced people, the conditions are not conducive to good health. According to a report published in 2013, there were "high levels of mortality, malnutrition, and measles" in the camp. Outbreaks of infectious diseases like measles are a constant concern in densely populated camps that often have poor sanitation. Malnutrition and limited access to health care can often become problematic when the local infrastructure is unable to sustain the population of the camp. Often the local administration and international agencies are overwhelmed by vast influxes of refugees during outbreaks of violence. Sufficient food, water, vaccines, and accommodations may be lacking. This can cause a public health disaster and lead to increased mortality. Refugee camps and camps for IDPs are one of the primary reasons that indirect mortality during a conflict can be so high.

Rwanda: Health Care for All

Rwanda, a small country in eastern Africa, came to the attention of the international community and world media in 1994 because of the Rwandan Genocide. In the span of just one hundred days, an estimated eight hundred thousand civilians were murdered. The genocide ended when rebel leader Paul Kagame seized control of the country. He later went on to become president of Rwanda. His tenure has been marred by the murder of opposition figures and journalists, as well as conflicts involving Rwandan soldiers in neighboring countries. But he also set about reforming the health care system of the country—one of the poorest in the world. This reform was hugely successful. According to Neal Emery in the *Atlantic*:

> Over the last ten years, Rwanda's health system development has led to the most dramatic improvements of health in history ... Deaths from HIV, TB, and malaria have each dropped by roughly 80 percent over the last decade and the maternal mortality ratio dropped by 60

percent over the same period. Even as the population has increased by 35 percent since 2000, the number of annual child deaths has fallen by 63 percent. In turn, these advances bolstered Rwanda's economic growth: GDP per person tripled to $580, and millions lifted themselves from poverty over the last decade

As Neal Emery points out, the cycle of poverty and ill health was reversed in Rwanda: improved public health helped spur economic development, rather than poor health slowing economic development.

The main driver of Rwanda's spectacular success was efforts to implement **universal health care**. Universal health care is when every person in a country is provided health care no matter their ability to pay. Most developed nations, including Canada and the United Kingdom, have universal health care. One exception is the United States, where 10 percent of the population is currently uninsured. A lack of health insurance means that a health shock can cause financial ruin or even an inability to pay for life-saving treatment. By contrast, in Rwanda everyone has access to health care that is not financially out of reach due to the country's implementation of universal health care. Of course, average life expectancy is much shorter in Rwanda than in developed countries, and the average spending per person on health care each year is just a fraction of what is spent in developed countries. But this increased spending in developed countries does not always lead to better outcomes. The American health care system struggles to retain patients in HIV treatment—nearly half of patients fail to continue treatment. This is very different in Rwanda where greater emphasis is placed on community outreach and making care affordable. Journalist Neal Emery writes that, "Rwanda retains 92 percent of patients in HIV care—compared to 50 percent in the U.S."

Rwanda's health care system is proof that even in poor countries universal health care is not out of reach. Everyone should have access to health care. When this fact is respected in a country, it leads to better health and faster economic development. In the future, there is hope that other countries can follow in Rwanda's footsteps and institute effective, equitable health care reform.

The Kalahari Desert stretches across parts of Namibia and Botswana.

5 Southern Africa

There are ten countries in southern Africa. The most populous and wealthiest country of the region is South Africa. South Africa has a checkered past. **Apartheid**, a system wherein black South Africans were oppressed by white South Africans, was enforced in the country for decades. That system ended in 1994 under the leadership of Nelson Mandela. In recent years, southern Africa has been stable and peaceful. The last major conflict, the Angolan civil war, which destabilized Angola for decades, ended in 2002. The government of Zimbabwe, led by President Robert Mugabe, is often criticized for human rights abuses inside Zimbabwe, but internal conflict has not spilled over its borders.

Southern Africa is the only region of Africa that is entirely south of the equator, meaning it is summer in November, December, and January rather than winter.

Health in Southern Africa

Health in southern Africa is typical of sub-Saharan Africa. Infectious diseases result in many more deaths than is typical in developed countries. High levels of maternal and child mortality result in markedly low average life expectancies, and high-quality health care is often inaccessible to large segments of the population. Southern Africa is also the epicenter of the global HIV/AIDS epidemic. While it is not the origin of HIV/AIDS, it is the region with the highest levels of the disease. This created a public health disaster in recent decades as the virus swept across the region. Today, average life expectancy in the small southern African countries of Swaziland and Lesotho is still the lowest in the world due to the terrible effects of HIV/AIDS and insufficient treatment for the disease.

Infectious Disease

The high incidence of HIV/AIDS is counterbalanced by some positive facts when it comes to infectious diseases in southern Africa. The southern tip of the continent lies at the extreme edge of malaria's historical range. The disease has actually been driven out of most of Lesotho and South Africa as well as parts of Namibia and Botswana through concerted malaria control efforts. Therefore, one of the deadliest diseases on the continent is absent from a significant part of southern Africa. Neglected tropical diseases also have a much lower incidence in the region, again because of its location away from the tropics. However, these positive factors do not outweigh the HIV/AIDS epidemic that has swept across the region and killed millions.

HIV/AIDS

HIV/AIDS is the leading cause of death in sub-Saharan Africa, and southern Africa is the epicenter of the epidemic. This is very different from developed nations, where it is not a common cause of death. (For example, HIV/AIDS is responsible for just 0.27 percent of deaths in the United States). This is because HIV/AIDS is much more common in sub-Saharan Africa than it is in any other region of the

The Origins of HIV

We know a great deal about the origin of HIV, but there are still many mysteries. Scientists have determined that HIV spread to humans from a species of chimpanzees in central and western Africa. This likely occurred when humans

HIV originated from SIV in a group of chimpanzees.

were exposed to blood from an SIV-infected chimpanzee while hunting or butchering the ape for meat. SIV (simian immunodeficiency virus) can infect many different simians (monkeys and apes), and this virus is what mutated into HIV. Yet human exposures to SIV had likely taken place for thousands of years during hunts. Why was it only in the twentieth century that HIV spread across the continent—and then the world—killing millions?

Researchers Amit Chitnis, Diana Rawls, and Jim Moore argue that the epidemic spread of HIV across the continent was aided by a number of colonial practices at the time:

- The widespread use of forced labor meant that farming was difficult, and, therefore, more bushmeat was eaten (and more opportunity for ape-to-human transmission presented itself).
- The rapid population growth in cities such as Kinshasa and Brazzaville created an ideal setting for an epidemic.
- The widespread vaccination campaigns of the time against diseases like smallpox and sleeping sickness could have spread the disease: syringes were reused at that time and no precautions were taken to stop the spread of blood-borne pathogens.
- Prostitution was encouraged in some labor camps, and some French officers and soldiers kept sex slaves.
- All of these factors made it more likely that HIV would become an epidemic and not simply an isolated outbreak as it likely was in the past.

world: 2.5 percent of people living in sub-Saharan Africa are HIV-positive. This number is even higher in southern Africa. In nine of the ten countries in southern Africa, more than 10 percent of adults are HIV-positive. The one exception is Angola. Additionally, fewer people living with HIV/AIDS in sub-Saharan Africa have access to treatment (or know they suffer from the disease). With treatment, it is now possible to live a long life after becoming HIV-positive. But without treatment, average life expectancy is approximately ten years after becoming HIV-positive.

"HIV" stands for "human immunodeficiency virus." Over a number of years, someone who is HIV-positive may develop acquired immunodeficiency syndrome (AIDS), although the progression to AIDS can often be stopped entirely by treatment. This is an important distinction to make when discussing HIV/AIDS: HIV is the virus itself, while AIDS is a cluster of symptoms that can result from HIV infection.

There are three stages to an HIV infection: acute infection, clinical latency, and AIDS. The acute infection occurs two to four weeks after the initial exposure to the virus. During this stage, symptoms resemble the flu and may include fever, sore throat, and headache. This stage lasts one to two weeks. However, some HIV-positive people do not experience any symptoms during this stage of the infection. The second stage, clinical latency, lasts ten years on average, but treatment can arrest the progress of the virus for much longer. There are no symptoms during clinical latency, and many people are not aware they are HIV-positive at this stage. Nevertheless, people in this stage are able to transmit the virus, and their immune system is being slowly compromised. The third stage is AIDS. At this point, one's immune system is severely compromised by the virus. Average life expectancy without treatment is just three years once one has reached this stage. One is at risk for **opportunistic infections** that are likely to prove fatal without treatment. By far the most common opportunistic infection in Africa is tuberculosis. According to the WHO, one-third of HIV-related deaths were due to TB. AIDS can also cause certain types of cancers that themselves result from viral infections, such as Kaposi's sarcoma.

HIV is spread through sexual intercourse and through blood, and from a pregnant mother to her unborn child. The majority of new infections today are from sexual intercourse: both heterosexual and homosexual intercourse can transmit HIV. Transmission via blood is the next most common cause of infection. This can happen through a number of different ways, including the sharing of needles during intravenous drug use, the transfusion of infected blood, and accidental needle stick injuries (usually involving medical personnel). The third and least common method of transmission is from mother to child during pregnancy. There is a significant risk that HIV is passed on to a child during pregnancy, and this risk increases if the child is breastfed since breast milk can contain the virus. In the past, some people mistakenly believed that HIV could be spread through other activities, such as kissing, sharing food or cups, or swimming in the same pool. However, these beliefs are false. Saliva is not infectious, and indirect contact with diluted blood—as might be possible in a swimming pool—is insufficient to transmit the virus.

There is no cure for HIV/AIDS, nor is there a vaccine. This means efforts to stop the spread of HIV/AIDS focus on the prevention of transmission. The WHO recommends a number of different ways to reduce the chance of transmission:

- Testing is one important way because nearly half of people with HIV do not know that they are HIV-positive. This is a major impediment to stopping the spread of HIV.

- The use of condoms during sexual intercourse is perhaps the single most important way to prevent the spread of HIV. This greatly reduces the chance of transmission. However, influential religious groups such as the Catholic Church oppose this measure on theological grounds.

- Making clean syringes available to drug users is recommended to prevent transmission through the sharing of needles during drug use, but this too is a political issue in some countries. In the United States, the use of federal money to fund needle exchanges (where drug users are provided with clean syringes in exchange for used ones) was banned until January 2016 due to the efforts of Republican lawmakers. Such bans increase the transmission of HIV by restricting the number of new syringes available to drug users and making it more likely they will share used ones.

Antiretroviral therapy (ART) is one means of prevention (and treatment) that is less religiously and politically controversial. If an HIV-positive person is receiving ART, it makes it much less likely HIV will be transmitted to a sexual partner. If a pregnant woman takes ART, it also makes it much more likely her child will not be HIV-positive.

The WHO recommends that all of these prevention methods be used simultaneously. While none of them can single-handedly stop the spread of HIV/AIDS, all together they have been used to lower the prevalence of HIV/AIDS in countries and regions around the world.

ART is also the standard treatment for HIV/AIDS. In addition to preventing transmission, it slows the rate at which an HIV infection progresses by preventing the virus from replicating. This lowers the levels of HIV virus in a person's body and makes the immune system stronger as a result. ART involves taking three or more antiretroviral medications: this is more effective than taking one medication alone. Even though ART is extremely effective at halting the progression of HIV infection, less than half of HIV-positive people are receiving ART. One reason for this is the fact that so many people do not know they are HIV-positive. But issues such as the cost of the medication and limited access to specialized health care services also play a role. However, millions of Africans do receive ART despite these problems, and great strides have been made in recent decades to make ART more affordable. At one time, treatment for one person over the course of a year cost $10,000. That number is now down to just $50 in some countries. New WHO guidelines about the delivery of ART to patients who are not able to regularly see a physician have also improved care for many patients in the developing world.

HIV/AIDS remains the greatest threat to public health in Africa. It was not long ago that the average life expectancy on the continent actually dropped during the 1990s due to the terrible toll of the virus. Around the rest of the world, average life expectancy surged due to advances in average income and medical care, but this could not offset the effects of HIV/AIDS in Africa, especially southern Africa. However, efforts to combat HIV/AIDS over the past decades have met with some success. According to the WHO, "Between 2000 and 2015, new HIV infections have fallen by 35%, [and] AIDS-related deaths have fallen by 28% with some 7.8 million lives saved."

Helminthiasis

Helminthiasis is the condition of having parasitic worms living in one's body (usually in the intestines). Tapeworms, roundworms, and hookworms are all different species of these parasites, but they are known as helminths in the medical field. The WHO considers two types of helminthiases to be neglected tropical diseases: soil-transmitted helminthiases and schistosomiasis (which is water-transmitted). Both diseases occur frequently in Africa although there are important differences between the two.

Soil-transmitted helminthiases include numerous different species of worms. Most soil-transmitted helminthiases spread when eggs in an infected person's feces contaminate the soil and nearby food and water, which is then consumed. However, there is one exception to this. Hookworm eggs hatch in the soil, and the worm then penetrates the exposed skin of a person who steps on it. According to the WHO, soil-transmitted helminthiases infect some 1.5 billion people—nearly one-quarter of the world's population. Infected people often have no symptoms when the case is not serious. When symptoms do occur, they include weakness, diarrhea, abdominal pain, and delayed physical and cognitive development in children.

Malnutrition can also result as the worms consume the person's food (and sometimes blood) and interfere with the absorption of some vitamins.

Schistosomiasis is caused by blood flukes (flatworms). These blood flukes live only their adult lives in humans. Their eggs hatch from the feces of infected people into water, where they infect freshwater snails. It is only later that the larvae leave the snails and reenter the water to penetrate the skin of a person who touches the contaminated water. Like soil-transmitted helminthiases, schistosomiasis can cause diarrhea and abdominal pain, but it can also cause more serious complications in advanced cases. It can result in liver and spleen enlargement, liver and kidney failure, and an increased risk of bladder cancer.

The treatment for soil-transmitted helminthiases and schistosomiasis is a simple course of oral medication. To control the spread of the diseases, the WHO recommends this medication be distributed to entire affected communities without even testing individuals to see who is infected. Nevertheless, hundreds of thousands of people die each year from helminthiasis. The fact that it is easy to treat does not change this. It is the most deadly neglected tropical disease.

Conflict and Health: Land Mines

After a conflict ends, people are not only left with physical and psychological scars. The land itself can be dangerous for generations to come because of the placement of land mines. Land mines are explosive devices that are designed to be concealed in the ground. When a person or vehicle goes over or near a land mine, it explodes. In war, land mines are used to prevent opposing troops from entering an area

A land mine in Libya

or to slow down an advancing army. But after a conflict
has ended, they often remain in the ground and continue
to kill and maim civilians who live nearby for generations.
The existence of mine fields can also slow economic growth
in a region by denying access to farmland and making the
transportation of goods dangerous. The UN estimates that
fifteen to twenty thousand people are killed each year by
land mines—the vast majority of them civilians. Many more
are maimed: loss of limb is common when one does survive
a land mine explosion.

George W. Bush and the Fight Against AIDS

Donor governments supply large amounts of money to combat the spread of HIV/AIDS around the world, although it is worth noting that the majority of funds used to combat HIV/AIDS come from domestic sources. By far the greatest foreign donor of money is the United States government— it provides more money to treat HIV/AIDS in developing countries than every other donor country in the world combined. This is largely due to the efforts of American president George W. Bush, who championed PEPFAR (President's Emergency Plan for AIDS Relief) in 2003. Since then, tens of billions of dollars have been spent to prevent, treat, and test for HIV/AIDS. As of 2015, PEPFAR was supplying antiretroviral treatment to a total of 9.5 million people according to the US government, and in 2015 alone mother-to-child transmission of the virus was prevented in 267,000 children due to the efforts of PEPFAR. The vast majority of people benefited by PEPFAR live in Africa, although PEPFAR is also active outside of Africa, in Vietnam and Haiti. PEPFAR is not without controversy; the program has religious undertones such as a focus on abstinence rather than condom use. But the fact is that

George W. Bush speaks on World AIDS Day.

it has helped slow the spread of HIV/AIDS, and supplying antiretroviral treatment to developing countries has changed millions of lives for the better.

Some efforts have been made to ban the use of land mines in recent years because of the threat they pose to civilians after a conflict ends. American president Bill Clinton was instrumental in creating the Ottawa Treaty (or Mine Ban Treaty) in 1997. Currently, 162 countries around the world are parties to the treaty that bans the future use of land mines, requires all mine fields to be removed, and forbids the stockpiling of land mines. However, thirty-five members of the UN are not parties to the treaty, including the United States. Fifty-one of the fifty-four countries in Africa are parties to the Ottawa Treaty—the exceptions are Morocco, Libya, and Egypt.

Angola, a country in southern Africa, is one of the worst affected countries on the continent. Angola was the scene of a bloody war for independence from 1961 to 1974. When Angolans campaigned for independence from the European country of Portugal, the Portuguese military responded with force and violence. The war dragged on thirteen years before Angola finally won its independence, but that was not the end of the violence. A civil war soon broke out between the rival parties that fought the Portuguese. The Angolan civil war lasted from 1975 until 2002. It was fueled by the Cold War as the United States and Soviet Union supported different armed groups. By the end of the war, Angola was one of the most heavily mined countries in the world. Today, there are still an estimated ten million land mines in the country. In 2010—eight years after the end of the war—eighty Angolans lost their lives to land mines. Most of the victims are children who are not only more likely to die from the blast of a land mine but are also more likely to trigger an explosion. According to the UN, the "small size, design and often colour [of land mines] make them very attractive to children, who may pick them up thinking they are toys."

While Angola is one of the countries that suffers the most from land mines, land mines are present in eleven African countries according to the International Campaign to Ban Landmines. Remnants of past conflicts, they continue to kill and maim civilians. Governments and NGOs do demine areas after conflicts end, but this is a lengthy and expensive process. The UN estimates that it costs between $300 and $1,000 to remove a single land mine. The best way to prevent future deaths and casualties is to prevent land mines from being laid in the first place. This is the focus of international efforts to halt the terrible cost of land mines on civilians.

South Africa: Brain Drain and Inequality

The state of health care in South Africa is in need of improvement, even according to government officials in the country. There exists a critical shortage of medical practitioners, like doctors and nurses. Additionally, there are great inequalities between the private health care system, used by those with financial means, and the public health care system, used by the majority of the population.

There is a crippling shortage of health care workers in South Africa and sub-Saharan Africa as a whole. While there are numerous reasons for this, one constant source of problems for health care in sub-Saharan Africa is **brain drain**. Brain drain refers to the situation when highly educated people, often medical professionals, emigrate from their home country to work in another country. This can lead to a shortage of medical practitioners as they immigrate to developed countries for better-paying jobs and a higher standard of living. Brain drain can have enormous consequences for a health care system. According to a report by S. Naicker:

> The already inadequate health systems of Africa, especially sub-Saharan Africa, have been badly damaged by the migration of their health professionals. There are 57 countries with a critical shortage of healthcare workers, a deficit of 2.4 million doctors and nurses. Africa has 2.3 healthcare workers per 1000 population, compared with the Americas, which have 24.8 healthcare workers per 1000 population. Only 1.3% of the world's health workers care for people who experience 25% of the global disease burden.

These numbers illustrate the magnitude of the problem.

In South Africa, inequalities between public and private health care also lead to worse public health. Those with private insurance receive better care, while those who do not have high-paying jobs receive inadequate care from an overburdened public health care system with a critical shortage of medical staff. Dr. Mphata Norman Mabasa, chairman of the South African Medical Association, describes this situation in a WHO report: "I've seen many instances of patients in the public health system dying when hospitals can't keep them longer. If you've got money, you can buy and save lives. In the public sector, for example, kidney dialysis is rationed." Long lines and wait times that last hours upon hours are another common complaint from those who have to use the public sector, while the private sector benefits from more doctors and more money. A report by the WHO found:

> Government spending on health care comprises less than half of total health expenditure even though the public system serves more than 80% of the population (i.e. around 40 million South Africans) without private health insurance. Around 70% of all doctors and most specialists only work in the private sector, the remaining 30% serve the public sector.

Brain drain exacerbates the inequalities between the private and public sectors.

The government of South Africa admits that these problems exist and is trying to solve them. In December of 2014, the government unveiled a plan to implement a national health insurance program over the next fourteen years. This would get rid of the distinction between private and public sectors, as all South Africans would have access to the same health care system. However, it remains to be seen whether or not this ambitious new plan will be funded or implemented in the future.

A drone delivers medical supplies.

The Future of Health in Africa

6

O ver the past decades, great strides have been made in improving health in Africa. Between the years of 1990 and 2015, the **Millennium Development Goals (MDGs)** guided international efforts to fight hunger, poverty, disease, poor health, and environmental degradation. These goals set lofty targets for improving health: a one-half reduction in the number of people who experience hunger, a two-thirds reduction in the under-five mortality rate, a three-quarters reduction in the maternal mortality rate, and decreasing the incidence and death rate of HIV/AIDS, malaria, and tuberculosis. While these goals were not met in every country in Africa in the twenty-five-year span of the MDGs, substantial improvements in public health were seen across the continent as a whole. A publication by the United Nations and African Union summarizes the gains that were made between 1990 and 2015 in the four MDGs relating to health:

> Africa excluding North Africa remains the most food-deficient of all regions of the world, with 25 per cent of its population having faced hunger and malnutrition during the 2011–2013 period, a modest 8 per cent improvement from the level experienced during the 1990–1992 period.
>
> ...

Continent-wide, the [under-five mortality rate] reduced from 146 deaths per 1,000 live births in 1990 to 65 deaths in 2012, i.e. a 55.5 per cent reduction against the target of a two-thirds reduction.

…

Africa has made progress in improving maternal health, although only Cabo Verde, Equatorial Guinea, Eritrea and Rwanda have reduced their maternal mortality ratio by more than 75 per cent between 1990 and 2013, hence meeting [the] MDG.

…

Efforts to combat HIV/AIDS, malaria and tuberculosis in Africa have yielded impressive results since 1990 and are placing the continent on a solid path to reversing the spread of these diseases. Indeed, a downward trend is observed in the incidence, prevalence and death rates associated with HIV/ AIDS, malaria and tuberculosis, especially since 2000.

As you can see, none of the MDGs were met in Africa as a whole, although improvements were seen in all four areas.

As African countries continue to tackle the issues of hunger, child and maternal mortality, and infectious diseases, health in Africa will change dramatically over the coming decades. There will be new challenges that the continent will face, but also new opportunities to increase life expectancy and expand access to health care services. We will examine some of the future challenges and opportunities that will soon reshape the health care sector of Africa.

Future Challenges

Noncommunicable Diseases

As life expectancy increases, the focus of health care in Africa will have to shift. Currently, health care is focused on the topics we have discussed, such as malnutrition, diarrheal diseases, neglected tropical diseases, respiratory tract infections, malaria, tuberculosis, and HIV/AIDS. In the future, as the impact of these diseases decreases, life expectancy will increase. Longer life will result in a whole new set of pressing public health concerns: noncommunicable diseases. These are the diseases that now confront developed countries: heart disease, diabetes, and cancer. It will be a major challenge for health care systems to pivot to fight these new diseases while still confronting the many infectious diseases that currently threaten public health on the continent.

Financing Health Care

Financing health care is currently one of the greatest challenges to public health in Africa. It is extremely difficult for developing countries to make affordable health care available to all of their citizens. Countries often struggle to raise significant revenue and must then make difficult decisions on how best to spend what money they do have. There have been some attempts to increase spending on health care, but there has been little progress on the issue. In 2001, all the member states of the AU pledged to spend 15 percent of their annual budgets on health care in the Abuja Agreement. But according to a report by the WHO in 2010, nearly every African country failed to hit this target.

In the future, sufficient financing for health care will continue to be a problem. The economies of African countries are growing quite rapidly, and this will lead to increased government revenue. However, this positive change will be tempered by decreasing levels of foreign aid to the continent. Foreign donor countries currently give substantial amounts of money to many African countries in order to improve public health, but this is slowly changing as many developed countries are trimming their own budgets. Humanitarian aid to developing countries is often one of the first expenses to be cut. This trend will likely continue in the future, and African countries will have to make up for this shortfall in their health care budgets.

Climate Change

It is a cruel twist of fate that Africa—the continent that has contributed the least to climate change—will be the continent that suffers the most from climate change. Greenhouse gases, mostly produced in developed countries, will cause the average temperature of the world to rise by an estimated 3.6 degrees Fahrenheit (1.5 degrees Celsius). While this may not sound like much, it will have a devastating effect on Africa. Drought and flooding will make farming on the continent less productive, leading to increased food insecurity and malnutrition than would otherwise occur. Increased rainfall and higher temperatures will accelerate the spread of vector-borne diseases as the range of mosquitos increase and they have more opportunity to breed. The heat itself will lead to more deaths from heat stress in areas that are already extremely hot. Floods in Africa are also expected to become more commonplace, causing deaths from the natural disaster itself as well as from contaminating water supplies with waste.

Climate change is one of the pressing issues of the modern world, and whether or not the international

Factories in Egypt release greenhouse gases.

community can successfully tackle it remains to be seen. What is certain is that Africa will bear the greatest burden from climate change despite playing little role in it. Some negative impact is already guaranteed by the current level of greenhouse gases. How extreme the impact is on Africa will be determined by the ability of the main drivers of climate change—the United States, EU member states, and China—to make concessions and limit the future production of greenhouse gases.

Future Opportunities

Technological Advances

E-Health—the integration of health services and technology—has huge potential in Africa. While technology allows us to communicate over great distances, this has not been fully integrated into modern health care. But that may soon change. Telemedicine, when patients are treated remotely by a distant health care professional, may make health care accessible to millions of Africans who live in remote areas. It may also help overcome the shortage of doctors in Africa if patients can be treated by doctors located on other continents. The African Development Bank discusses the possible advantages of e-Health in the following way:

> Harnessing e-Health will help overcome the triple challenges of inadequate access, finance, and human resources by delivering high-quality healthcare services to all citizens, even in remote areas. e-Health can also contribute to greater transparency and accountability in health services, by promoting evidence-based practice and error reduction, diagnostic accuracy and treatment. e-Health will also empower users, enabling better self-care and decision making. It can also be promoted to shift tasks down the skills ladder as appropriate, thereby helping to address skills shortages. Finally, e-Health has the potential to increase cost-efficiency by streamlining processes, reducing waiting times, and improving data accuracy. In sum, the e-Health revolution can help to address

the major shortages in human resources and access and therefore provides a very positive outlook for African countries in the years to come.

Already, patients in African hospitals are being diagnosed by doctors in India. However, there is still huge potential for growth in this field. It remains to be seen when e-Health will become more widespread around the world and in Africa. Yet it is one of the great hopes for improving health care on the continent.

The Eradication of Diseases

As we have learned, smallpox was eradicated in the past through an aggressive campaign of vaccinations. While there were hopes that other diseases would soon follow, this has not been the case. It has been four decades since smallpox occurred naturally, and it remains the only human disease to be fully eradicated. However, it is likely that some other diseases may one day be eradicated as well. The most likely candidates are polio and guinea worm disease. In 2015, there were just seventy-four cases of naturally occurring polio in the entire world. They were restricted to two countries: Afghanistan and Pakistan (where the security situation makes vaccinations difficult).

Likewise, in 2015 there were only 22 cases of guinea worm disease, down from 3.5 million in 1984. Once a neglected tropical disease that took a terrible toll on public health in twenty African countries, guinea worm disease is on its last leg in just four countries. It will almost certainly be eradicated soon. In the future, it is hoped that other neglected tropical diseases and even major diseases like malaria will also be eradicated. This would represent a huge step forward for public health in Africa and around the world. The eradication of these diseases becomes ever more likely as more vaccines are developed and access to health care and preventative measures improve.

Advances in Research

One of the most promising opportunities for health in Africa is groundbreaking medical research. According to a report by advisory firm KPMG:

> "Advances in chemistry will save and improve lives, as researchers develop drugs specifically for Africa, or at least for low income societies. One good example is the retroviral treatment developed by Indian pharmaceutical company Cipla: unlike previous drug cocktails, Cipla's fixed-dose combination does not require refrigeration, which played an important part in prompting its uptake in Africa. If heat resistant insulin is ever developed, for instance, it is certain that its effect in Africa will be tremendous"

In addition to new drug formulations like Cipla, new vaccines and treatments may soon radically alter the landscape of public health in Africa. A cure for HIV/AIDS or a vaccine to prevent the disease could save millions of lives. A new vaccine for malaria or a more effective vaccine for tuberculosis would also save many lives and reshape public health. Currently, there is ongoing scientific research in all of these areas and dozens of new vaccines are undergoing clinical trials to test their efficacy and side effects. Just one successful trial could change the future of health care in Africa.

Delivery Drones in Rwanda

One technology that may revolutionize health care on the continent is drones. These small unmanned aircraft were expected to begin delivering blood and medical supplies to clinics and hospitals around Rwanda in the summer of 2016. In partnership with the Rwandan government, the American company Zipline is at the center of these efforts. Journalist Rohini Nambiar describes how the system will work:

> Doctors can place their request for medical supplies through a text message and the supplies are dispatched from a hub, located next to a medical warehouse facility, to remote regions within minutes. Each battery-powered drone, named the Zip, is able to carry up to 1.5kg of medical supplies and can fly a distance of more than 120km. The Zip operates through a slingshot mechanism and the supplies are dropped at their destination using a parachute.

> Zipline's project with the Rwandan government is set to launch in July this year to deliver blood supplies across the country. The use of drones to deliver essential medical supplies is expected to reduce the delivery time from 15 hours to 15 minutes, according to Zipline.

This ability to quickly deliver medical supplies to remote clinics and hospitals situates drones to improve access to health care across Africa. If the project goes well in Rwanda, Zipline plans to expand into other African countries.

The Sustainable Development Goals: Hope for the Future

The Millennium Development Goals lapsed in 2015. They were not met in many countries in Africa, but public health improved across the continent as a whole, nevertheless. The Sustainable Development Goals have now replaced the Millennium Development goals. These goals are to be met by 2030, and they offer an ambitious vision of improving health around the world. Two of the seventeen goals are to end all forms of malnutrition and to make safe, affordable drinking water available to everyone. If these goals are met, they will revolutionize the state of public health in Africa and many other regions of the world. Malnutrition is involved in half of childhood deaths, and it perpetuates a cycle of poverty and ill health throughout the developing world. Access to clean drinking water would be an important step in reducing diarrheal diseases—a leading cause of death in children—as well as many neglected tropical diseases that are spread through contaminated water and leave millions disabled or dead in their wake.

Sustainable Development Goal number three concerns public health directly, not malnutrition or drinking water. It reads, "ensure healthy lives and promote well-being for all at all ages." This goal sets a number of targets that can be measured, such as reducing the "the global maternal mortality ratio to less than 70 per 100,000 live births" and "under-5 mortality to at least as low as 25 per 1,000 live births." Additionally, it calls for universal health care for everyone and "by 2030, end the epidemics of AIDS, tuberculosis, malaria and neglected tropical diseases and combat hepatitis, water-borne diseases and other communicable diseases." If these goals are achieved, public health in Africa will be radically different than it is today. As we have seen, high rates of maternal and child mortality cause millions of preventable deaths each year on the continent. Lack of access to health care likewise results in high numbers of death and disability, and the scourge of infectious diseases like HIV/AIDS, tuberculosis, and malaria affects Africa in ways that are unparalleled in developed countries.

Whether or not the Sustainable Development Goals are met in the coming years depends on the factors that we have looked at in this chapter. The challenges of dwindling foreign aid for health care, climate change, and the rising impact of noncommunicable diseases will tax health care systems around Africa. But there is reason for optimism as well. The eradication of some diseases like polio and guinea worm disease are on the horizon. Others may soon follow. Advances in medical research and technology may also change public health in ways that we cannot even conceive of at the moment. The governments of Africa and NGOs are optimistic about the future of the continent. If the Sustainable Development Goals are met, it will be the first time in human history that poverty and ill health are largely eliminated. The timeline of fifteen years is ambitious, but with concerted effort and technological advances, it may be possible. Public health in Africa has made rapid gains in the last twenty-five years, and more are sure to follow. The one certainty is that the future of health in Africa will look very different than it does today as development continues.

Regional Map
of Africa

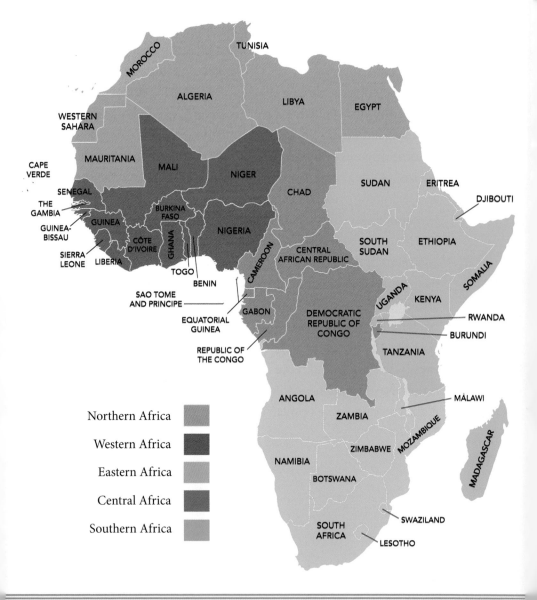

TUNISIA

MOROCCO

ALGERIA

LIBYA

EGYPT

WESTERN
SAHARA

CAPE
VERDE

MAURITANIA

MALI

NIGER

SUDAN

ERITREA

DJIBOUTI

SENEGAL

THE
GAMBIA

GUINEA-
BISSAU

GUINEA

BURKINA
FASO

CHAD

CÔTE
D'IVOIRE

GHANA

NIGERIA

SIERRA
LEONE

LIBERIA

TOGO

BENIN

CAMEROON

CENTRAL
AFRICAN REPUBLIC

SOUTH
SUDAN

ETHIOPIA

SOMALIA

SAO TOME
AND PRINCIPE

EQUATORIAL
GUINEA

GABON

DEMOCRATIC
REPUBLIC OF
CONGO

UGANDA

KENYA

RWANDA

BURUNDI

REPUBLIC OF
THE CONGO

TANZANIA

ANGOLA

MALAWI

ZAMBIA

MOZAMBIQUE

MADAGASCAR

ZIMBABWE

NAMIBIA

BOTSWANA

SWAZILAND

SOUTH
AFRICA

LESOTHO

Northern Africa

Western Africa

Eastern Africa

Central Africa

Southern Africa

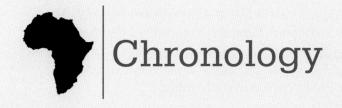

Chronology

1492 Christopher Columbus arrives in the Americas—he brings diseases from Europe and takes home diseases from the Americas

1526 A Portuguese ship transports African slaves to the Americas for the first time

1796 The smallpox vaccine is invented by Edward Jenner

1872 The suspected year of the jigger fleas' introduction to Africa when a ship from Brazil dumps sand used to balance the ship off the coast of western Africa

1903 David Bruce identifies the protozoa that causes sleeping sickness

1945 The UN is founded after World War II

1951 Max Theiler becomes the first African to win a Nobel Prize for his medical research regarding yellow fever

1959 Preserved blood from a Congolese man in this year offers the first physical evidence for the existence of HIV/AIDS

1961 The Angolan War of Independence begins against Portugal

1963 The African Union is founded

1969 A young man dies from a mysterious illness in St. Louis, Missouri; years later, it is determined that he is the first known victim of AIDS in North America

1972 The Ebola virus is first identified

1974 The Angolan War of Independence ends

1975 The Angolan civil war begins

1976 The first outbreaks of Ebola virus disease occur in the DRC and South Sudan

1977 Smallpox becomes the first disease to be eradicated by a global campaign

1979 Malaria is eradicated in Tunisia

1991 Earvin "Magic" Johnson, a professional basketball player, publically announces that he is HIV-positive and becomes an activist to prevent the spread of HIV/AIDS; the Sierra Leone civil war begins

1994 The Rwandan Genocide occurs over the course of one hundred days; apartheid ends in South Africa

1998 The Second Congo War begins

2000 The Millennium Development Goals are established

2001 The Abuja Agreement is signed—members of the AU pledge to commit 15 percent of their government's budget to health care

2002 The Sierra Leone civil war ends, leaving thousands with disabling injuries in its wake; the Angolan civil war ends

2003 The Second Congo War ends after an estimated 5.4 million deaths; PEPFAR begins

2004 The Milwaukee Protocol is first used to successfully treat a patient infected with rabies

2011 South Sudan becomes the world's newest country

2013 The West African Ebola virus epidemic begins

2014 South Africa unveils a fourteen-year implementation plan for national health insurance

2015 A vaccine-preventable measles outbreak in the DRC kills 450 people; the timeline for the Millennium Development Goals ends

2016 Rwanda intends to use drones to deliver medical supplies to remote clinics and hospitals

Glossary

African Union (AU) A continental union of every country in Africa except Morocco.

antiretroviral therapy (ART) A combination of drugs that slows the progression of HIV.

apartheid A government-enforced system of racial segregation in South Africa.

Arab Spring A series of democratic protests that began in 2010 and spread across northern Africa and the Middle East.

brain drain The emigration of highly trained professionals from one country to another.

developed countries Countries with high average incomes and high life expectancies.

developing countries Countries with relatively low average incomes and life expectancies when compared to developed countries.

displaced people People who are forced to leave their homes (usually due to conflict).

e-health The use of technology to support health care.

endemic Commonly found (in a location).

extreme poverty Defined as living on just $1.90 a day.

generic A class of medications that are identical to their brand-name equivalents but offered at a lower price after the patent of the brand-name drug has expired.

health shock An unpredictable illness.

indirect deaths Deaths resulting from a conflict that are not due to actual violence.

internally displaced person Someone who is forced to leave their home but remains in their home country.

measles A vaccine-preventable disease that is particularly dangerous for the malnourished and the young.

Millennium Development Goals (MDGs) Eight goals to reduce poverty, mortality, and environmental degradation between the years of 1990 and 2015.

mortality rate The number of deaths in a given population; it's usually expressed as number of deaths per thousand people due to a specific cause.

neglected tropical diseases A group of infectious diseases that primarily affect people living in poverty in tropical and subtropical climates.

noncommunicable diseases Diseases that are not spread from person to person, such as heart disease and cancer.

nongovernmental organization (NGO) A not-for-profit organization that is often charitable or political in nature.

opportunistic infection In people living with AIDS, it is an infection that is made possible due to a weakening of the immune system.

out-of-pocket health payment A payment for medical care that is made by the individual (not an insurance company or government).

per capita GDP Calculated by dividing the total value of goods and services produced in a country by the population (in a given time period); it is a measure of the average income a person in a country has.

postpartum After birth; used to describe conditions that result from childbirth.

post-traumatic stress disorder (PTSD) A mental disorder caused by a traumatic experience; symptoms often include nightmares and flashbacks of the experience.

primary health care (PHC) Essential health care that is available in the community when someone first seeks medical help.

prognosis The predicted course of disease including the likelihood of survival.

prophylaxis A preventative measure to control the spread of a disease.

protozoa A type of unicellular organism; some are parasites that are responsible for a number of diseases, including malaria.

tuberculosis (TB) A bacterial infectious disease that usually affects the lungs.

universal health care Health care that is accessible to everyone.

vaccine A pharmaceutical product (often an injection) that prevents an infectious disease or minimizes its effects.

vector A living organism that spreads a disease.

World Health Organization (WHO) An agency of the United Nations that aims to improve people's health around the world.

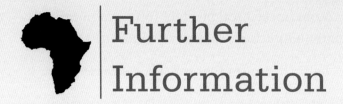

Further Information

Books

Allen, Arthur. *Vaccine: The Controversial Story of Medicine's Greatest Lifesaver*. New York, NY: W. W. Norton & Company, 2007.

Foege, William H. *House on Fire: The Fight to Eradicate Smallpox*. Berkeley, CA: University of California Press, 2011.

Shah, Sonia. *The Fever: How Malaria Has Ruled Mankind for 50,000 Years*. New York, NY: Picador, 2010.

Websites

Map of Vaccine-Preventable Outbreaks
http://www.cfr.org/interactives/GH_Vaccine_Map/
This website includes an interactive map of all recorded vaccine-preventable outbreaks from 2008 to the present.

Millennium Development Goals Progress Visualization
http://vizhub.healthdata.org/mdg/
A website that creates a visualization for every country's progress toward meeting the MDGs related to health.

The Sustainable Development Goals

http://www.un.org/sustainabledevelopment/

The official UN website for the Sustainable Development Goals includes historical facts and figures as well as precise numbers about future goals to improve public health around the world.

Videos

Imagining a New Future for Health Systems in Africa

https://www.ted.com/watch/ted-institute/ted-bcg/mathieu-lamiaux-imagining-a-new-future-for-health-systems-in-africa

Health care consultant Mathieux Lamiuex outlines the past progress of public health in Africa as well as future opportunities.

World-Class Health Care

https://www.ted.com/talks/ernest_madu_on_world_class_health_care

Cardiologist Ernest Madu discusses the need for better treatment of cardiovascular disease in Africa.

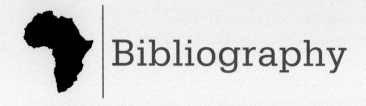

Bibliography

African Development Bank. "Health in Africa over the Next Fifty Years." March 2013. http://www.afdb.org/fileadmin/uploads/afdb/Documents/Publications/Economic_Brief_-_Health_in_Africa_Over_the_Next_50_Years.pdf.

Andersen, Ted. "WHO Approves World's First-Ever Dengue Vaccine." *Time*, April 15, 2016. http://time.com/4296193/who-dengue-vaccine/.

Baron, David. "Can a Gabonese Director Cure the Albert Schweitzer Hospital?" BBC News, July 19, 2012. http://www.bbc.com/news/world-africa-18120920.

"Bridging the Gap in South Africa." *Bulletin of the World Health Organization* 88, no. 11 (November 2010): pp. 797–876. http://www.who.int/bulletin/volumes/88/11/10-021110/en/.

CDC. "Outbreaks Chronology: Ebola Virus Disease." Retrieved July 11, 2016. http://www.cdc.gov/vhf/ebola/outbreaks/history/chronology.html.

Chitnis, Amit, Diana Rawls, and Jim Moore. "Origin of HIV Type 1 in Colonial French Equatorial Africa?" *AIDS Research and Human Retroviruses* 16, no. 1 (2000): pp. 5–8.

Doctors Without Borders. "At Obama-Modi Meeting in New York, MSF Urges India to Protect Affordable Medicines for Millions." September 28, 2015. http://www

.doctorswithoutborders.org/article/obama-modi-meeting-
new-york-msf-urges-india-protect-affordable-medicines-
millions.

Donnelly, John. "Polio: A Fight in a Lawless Land." *Boston
Globe*, February 27, 2006. http://archive.boston.com/
yourlife/health/diseases/articles/2006/02/27/polio_a_fight_
in_a_lawless_land/.

Emery, Neal. "Rwanda's Historic Health Recovery: What the
U.S. Might Learn." *Atlantic*, February 20, 2013. http://www.
theatlantic.com/health/archive/2013/02/rwandas-historic-
health-recovery-what-the-us-might-learn/273226/.

Ford, Nathan, Alexandra Calmy, and Edward J. Mills.
"The First Decade of Antiretroviral Therapy in Africa."
Globalization and Health 7, no. 33 (2011): pp. 1–6.

Geneva Declaration Secretariat. *Global Burden of Armed
Violence*. September 2008. http://www.genevadeclaration.
org/fileadmin/docs/Global-Burden-of-Armed-Violence-
full-report.pdf.

KPMG. *The State of Healthcare in Africa*. 2012. https://
www.kpmg.com/Africa/en/IssuesAndInsights/Articles-
Publications/Documents/The-State-of-Healthcare-in-
Africa.pdf.

Lecky, Muhammed M., and Tunde Segun. "Improving
Primary Health Care in Nigeria: What's Needed Now."
Impatient Optimist, September 24, 2015. http://www.
impatientoptimists.org/Posts/2015/09/Whats
-Needed-to-Improve-Nigerias-Primary-Health-Care
-System.

Maco, Vicente, Manuel Tantaleán, and Eduardo Gotuzzo. "Evidence of Tungiasis in Pre-Hispanic America." *Emerging Infectious Diseases* 17, no. 5 (2011): pp. 855–862.

Murray, Natasha Evelyn Anne, Mikkel B. Quam, and Annelies Wilder-Smith. "Epidemiology of Dengue: Past, Present and Future Prospects." *Clinical Epidemiology* 5 (2013): pp. 299–309.

Naicker, S., J. Plange-Rhule, R. C. Tutt, and J. B. Eastwood. "Shortage of Healthcare Workers in Developing Countries—Africa." *Ethnicity & Disease* 19, S1 (2009): pp. 60–64.

Nambiar, Rohini. "How Rwanda Is Using Drones to Save Millions of Lives." CNBC, May 27, 2016. http://www.cnbc.com/2016/05/27/how-rwanda-is-using-drones-to-save-millions-of-lives.html.

Newson, Linda. "Pathogens, Places and Peoples." In *Technology, Disease and Colonial Conquests, Sixteenth to Eighteenth Centuries*, edited by George Raudzens. pp. 167–210. Boston, MA: Brill, 2001.

Oxford Business Group. "Tunisian Health Sector to Undergo Overhaul." Retrieved June 21, 2016. http://www.oxfordbusinessgroup.com/overview/annual-check-solid-foundation-sector-ready-overhaul.

Polonsky, Jonathan A., Axelle Ronsse, Iza Cigleneki, Monica Rull, and Klaudia Porten. "High Levels of Mortality, Malnutrition, and Measles, Among Recently-displaced Somali Refugees in Dagahaley Camp, Dadaab Refugee Camp Complex, Kenya, 2001." *Conflict and Health* 7, no. 1 (2013): p. 1–9.

Prüss-Üstün, A., J. Wolf, C. Corvalán, R. Bos, and M. Neira. *Preventing Disease Through Healthy Environments: A Global Assessment of the Burden of Disease from Environmental Risks*. Geneva, Switzerland: World Health Organization, 2016.

Rosenberg, Tina. "In Rwanda, Health Care Coverage That Eludes the U.S." *New York Times*, July 3, 2012. http://opinionator.blogs.nytimes.com/2012/07/03/rwandas-health-care-miracle/?_r=1.

Schneider, William H. "Smallpox in Africa during Colonial Rule." *Medical History* 53, no. 2 (2009): pp. 193–227.

Scoones, Ian. *The Politics of Trypanosomiasis Control in Africa*. Brighton, UK: STEPS Centre, 2014.

Singh, Sunit K., and Daniel Ruzek, eds. *Viral Hemorrhagic Fevers*. CRC Press, 2013.

Snow, Robert W., Punam Amratia, Caroline W. Kabaria, Abdisalan M. Noor, and Kevin Marsh. "The Changing Limits and Incidence of Malaria in Africa: 1939–2009." *Advances in Parasitology* 78 (2012): pp. 169–262.

UN. "Demining." Retrieved June 30, 2016. http://www.un.org/en/globalissues/demining/.

UN Economic Commission for Africa. *MDG Report 2015: Assessing Progress in Africa Toward the Millennium Development Goals*. September 2015. http://www.undp.org/content/undp/en/home/librarypage/mdg/mdg-reports/africa-collection.html.

Villaveces, Andrés, Etienne Krug, Alex Butchart, and Gyanendra K. Sharma. *Small Arms and Global Health.* Geneva, Switzerland: World Health Organization, 2001.

WHO. "Tuberculosis: Fact Sheet." Retrieved June 30, 2016. http://www.who.int/mediacentre/factsheets/fs104/en/.

WHO. "Tuberculosis Vaccine Development." Retrieved June 30, 2016. http://www.who.int/immunization/research/development/tuberculosis/en/.

WHO. "Water Sanitation Health." Retrieved June 30, 2016. http://www.who.int/water_sanitation_health/diseases/malnutrition/en/.

WHO. *The World Health Report: 2001: Mental Health: New Understanding, New Hope.* 2001. http://www.who.int/whr/2001/en/whr01_en.pdf?ua=1.

WHO. *World Malaria Report 2015.* 2015. http://apps.who.int/iris/bitstream/10665/200018/1/9789241565158_eng.pdf?ua=1.

World Bank. *Clean and Improved Cooking in Sub-Saharan Africa.* November 2014. http://www-wds.worldbank.org/external/default/WDSContentServer/WDSP/IB/2015/08/18/090224b08307b414/4_0/Rendered/PDF/Clean0and0impr000a0landscape0report.pdf.

Index

Page numbers in **boldface** are illustrations. Entries in **boldface** are glossary terms.

Great Pyramids, **8**

health care, access to, 6, 12–13, 22–25, 29, 31, 39–41, 46, 54, 58, 62, 78–79, 81, 85, 88, 96–97, 100–102, 106
health shock, 59
helminthiasis, 89–90
HIV/AIDS, 5, 11, 12, 15–16, 18, 29, 32, 41, 45, 48–49, 64–65, 68, 77–78, 82–89, 92–93, 99–101, 106, 108–109

India, and drugs, 65–66
indirect deaths, 53–55
infectious diseases, 15–20, 32–37, 48–53, 64–74, 81–90, 100, 109
internally displaced person, 74–76

Kalahari Desert, **80**

land mines, 90–95, **91**
Libya, 9, 12–13, 22, 24, 94
life expectancy, 12, 15, 25, 29, 40, 43, 62, 78, 81–82, 85, 100–101

Maalin, Ali Maow, 62–64, **63**
malaria, 5, 12, 14–16, 24, 29, 32, 41, 48, 64–70, 72,

77, 82, 99–101, 105–106, 108–109
malnutrition/hunger, 5–6, 12, 14, 29–30, 32–34, 40, 43, 46, 48–49, 54, 58, 62, 68, 76, 90, 99, 101–102, 108
measles, 47, 76
Millennium Development Goals, 99–100, 108
mortality rate, 5, 48, 54, 77
child/infant, 5, 12–14, 29, 43, 46, 59, 61–62, 81, 99–100, 108–109
maternal, 5, 12–13, 29, 31, 40, 43, 45–46, 61–62, 81, 99–100, 108–109
mosquitos/mosquito nets, 66–69, **67**, **71**, 72–74, 102

neglected tropical diseases, 6, 19–20, 43, 48, 51, 82, 89, 101, 105, 108
Nigeria, 6, 22, 29, 31–32, 39–41
noncommunicable diseases, 14–15, 101, 109
nongovernmental organization (NGO), 39, 45, 47–48, 59, 62, 95, 109
northern Africa, 9–25, 27, 29, 32

opportunistic infection, 86

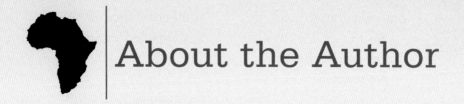

About the Author

Derek L. Miller is a writer and educator from Salisbury, Maryland. His books include *The Economy in Contemporary Africa* and *Earth, Sun, and Moon: Cyclic Patterns of Lunar Phases, Eclipses, and the Seasons*. When he's not reading, researching, teaching, or writing, Miller enjoys traveling. He hopes to visit Africa soon, though the prospect of picking a country—or even a region—has proven overwhelming.